Popular Mechanics

THE BOY CAMPER

Popular Mechanics

THE BOY CAMPER

160 OUTDOOR PROJECTS AND ACTIVITIES

HEARST BOOKS
A division of Sterling Publishing Co., Inc.

New York / London
www.sterlingpublishing.com

Library of Congress Cataloging-in-Publication Data
Popular mechanics : the boy camper : 200 outdoor projects & activities / the editors of Popular mechanics.
    p. cm.
"The projects in this book were created nearly 100 years ago"--T.p. verso.
ISBN-13: 978-1-58816-703-3
ISBN-10: 1-58816-703-8
1. Camping. 2. Outdoor life. 3. Outdoor recreation for children.
I. Popular mechanics (Chicago, Ill. : 1959) II. Title: Boy camper.
GV191.7.P66 2008
796.54—dc22

                                                                    2007029692

10   9   8   7   6   5   4   3   2   1

Book design by Barbara Balch

Published by Hearst Books
A Division of Sterling Publishing Co., Inc.
387 Park Avenue South, New York, NY 10016

Popular Mechanics and Hearst Books are trademarks
of Hearst Communications, Inc.
www.popularmechanics.com
For information about custom editions, special sales, premium and corporate purchases, please contact Sterling Special Sales Department at 800-805-5489 or specialsales@sterlingpub.com.

Distributed in Canada by Sterling Publishing
c/o Canadian Manda Group, 165 Dufferin Street
Toronto, Ontario, Canada M6K 3H6

Distributed in Australia by Capricorn Link (Australia) Pty. Ltd.
P.O. Box 704, Windsor, NSW 2756 Australia

Manufactured in China

Sterling ISBN 13: 978-1-58816-703-3
        ISBN 10: 1-58816-703-8

CONTENTS

IN-TENTS CONCENTRATION

CHAPTER 2

CAMPSITE BASICS *67*

MASTERING THE GREAT OUTDOORS

OUTDOOR INNOVATIONS

CATCHING *the* BIG ONE *88*

ANGLING FOR A WINNER

THE REEL DEAL

TERRIFIC TACKLE BOX

THE PERFECT FLY

CLEANING THE CATCH

CHAPTER 4

THE BOATING LIFE *160*

WHAT'S CANOE?

PADDLE POWER

POWER PLAY

FLOATING IMPROVEMENTS

CHAPTER 5

THE REMARKABLE MARKSMAN *219*

THE WOODSMAN ARCHER

CAMPFIRE GRUB *233*

HOME ON THE RANGE

CAMP KITCHEN GADGETS

THE OPEN-AIR FEAST

OUTDOOR KITCHEN APPLIANCES

FOREWORD

Remember those great summertime camping trips from your childhood? How the days stretched out into forever as you explored a dappled sunlit path under a canopy of tall trees or felt the chill of the water when you first dipped your toe into the lake? There was something special, and perhaps a little magical, about cooking a meal over an open fire and discovering where the fish were hiding in a shaded swimming spot.

To pay tribute to a time when every boy knew how to bait a hook, we've assembled this collection of outdoor activities from long ago. But don't let appearances deceive you—there's still a lot worth learning from all this time-tested wisdom.

Tying a lure and learning how to cast a fly haven't changed much even as rod technology has improved. The goal is still to find the fish, hook it, and bring it back to the campsite before dinner. And of course cooking out in the open is still the rewarding tasty delight it has always been. So we've included a few choice fishing projects as well as ideas for outdoor gadgets and appliances to help keep everyone well-fed. You'll also find amazing boat-building plans and advice for making the most of your time on the water. Even if a boy never builds his own sailing canoe, reading about it is fine entertainment.

Today's campers will be amused by some of the ways yesterday's adventurers kept themselves busy. From the fascinating making a bed of boughs to the fantastic building a log cabin, boys will find a panorama of outdoor activities represented here. We've covered the basics of making a temporary or permanent camp structure and fundamental skills such as archery, as well as lesser-known secrets for taking advantage of winter camping activities.

So no matter where or what season a boy is looking to set up camp, he'll find a whole new world to explore in the pages of this book.

The Editors
Popular Mechanics

{ CHAPTER 1 }

CAMPGROUND SHELTER

SUPER STRUCTURES

— BUILD YOUR OWN SIMPLE LOG CABIN —

A picturesque year-round cabin of logs, a weekend house, or a permanent hunting and fishing camp far off beaten trails can be yours at very little cost if you follow this simple method of construction. If you're fairly handy at building a masonry foundation and handling a hammer and saw, you can do the whole job yourself, because there are no heavy materials and no tricky saddle-notched corners such as are found in the conventional log cabin. Here the logs are halved and edged as in *Figure 1* and assembled vertically, "stockade" fashion, which makes it possible to use small logs from second-growth timber such as aspen and poplar. Although these timbers do not endure for long when laid

horizontally, either will be entirely satisfactory when placed vertically because there are no crevices to catch and hold moisture. Placing the logs vertically also does away with the messy and difficult job of chinking.

Preparing the logs: Logs should preferably be cut during the late fall or early winter so that they may have at least six months to season. As soon as they are cut they should be taken to the mill and split, edged and peeled. A peeled log can be treated more surely to resist decay and insects. The split logs should be coated thoroughly with boiled linseed oil thinned with a little turpentine and applied warm with a soft brush. After the first coat has dried for two weeks or more, a single coat of pure linseed oil should be applied. A third coat may be applied after the cabin is completed. Logs in contact with the earth should be painted with a preservative

solution before being placed. It's also wise to use preservative on the sills and floor joists.

The foundation: Having chosen your site carefully in regard to drainage, water supply, view, etc., level the surface of the ground and mark out the locations of the walls and fireplace, *Figures 7* and *8*. Then dig the foundation trench about 3 ft. deep and 16 or 18 in. wide. Excavate the space for the fireplace also. Square the sides of the trench neatly and you will not need a form up to the grade level. The footing should be about 6 to 8 in. deep and should cover the fireplace area as well. Use a mixture of 1 part cement, 2 parts sand, and 3 parts gravel. Once the footing has set, continue the wall about 1 ft. above the grade, using wood forms.

If native rocks are handy, an attractive wall can be built by incorporating these with the cement, *Figure 7*. While the concrete is soft, long bolts or rods threaded at the top are embedded in the mixture at regular intervals to provide anchors for the plates. Care must be taken to have the plates perfectly level. Large rocks are packed into the fireplace pit on top of the footing already laid, *Figures 10* and *11*. This layer will bring the level up to about 18 in. from the surface. Top this with a layer of sand and then pour on 6 in. of concrete. Add a 1-ft. layer of small stones and cover with

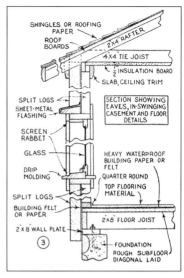

"STOCKADE" WALLS OF VERTICAL SPLIT LOGS DO AWAY WITH CHINKING AND SADDLE-NOTCHING.

concrete up to the grade level. Use selected rocks laid in courses to bring the fireplace foundation up to the height of the walls.

Leave the work at this stage until later. Two or more vents should be left in the foundation wall to allow ventilation beneath the floor. These openings should be covered with fine-mesh wire netting.

The framework: After the plates have been bolted to the foundation, the sills and joists are put on as shown in *Figures 1, 3,* and *9*. Note that the

outside edge of the sills is flush with the outside surface of the foundation walls. The joists are spaced 16 in. on center. Corner posts are installed next to hold the framework, *Figure 9*. These are made up from a single 4 by 4-in. upright with a 2 by 4-in. and a 2 by 6-in. upright spiked on it, *Figure 1*. Now the subfloor, of ¾-in. unmatched boarding, is laid over the joists in the diagonal position shown. The framework pieces to which the outside vertical logs are spiked are next nailed in place. These horizontals are fastened to the corner posts at a height of 8 ft. above the floor and held solid by temporary braces on one side and on the other by the two uprights on either side of the door, *Figure 9*. The 4 by 4-in. tie joists are now placed in position spaced about 2½ ft. apart. Use diagonal braces to keep this frame square and true until the outside logs are nailed on.

Lastly, a 2 by 4-in. plate is nailed to the floor flush with the outside edge all around except across the door openings. Later the inside logs will be toenailed to this plate, *Figure 1A*.

The split-log walls: The frame is now ready for the outside logs. Starting at one of the front corners, two 9-ft. lengths of heavy building paper or felt are stretched between the top frame and the sill. The first length is carried around the corner about 10 in. and tacked on. The second piece overlaps the first, making a weatherproof corner. Locate the first

log with the vertical edge flush with the corner post. The lower end should extend down over the sill and cover a few inches of the stonework, *Figure 1B*. It is then spiked to the sill, wall plates and the top frame.

Continue nailing the logs in place, working toward a doorway, hanging sheets of building paper ahead of the logs. As you approach the window opening, nail the frame in place against the door uprights, *Figure 9*. Then, using short logs cut to length, place them in under the window and nail the frame to them. Begin at the center with the longest split log on the end opposite the fireplace. This supports the ridge pole and should be located in the exact center of the wall. Of course, a length of building paper is first stretched from the nailing joist to the sill.

Finish from the center log to the corners, running the paper only up

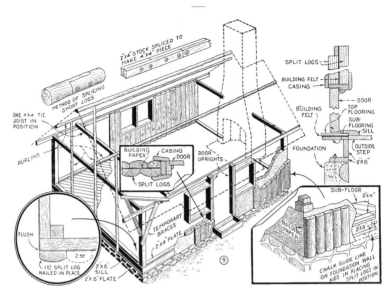

to the nailing joist. After the end wall is completed, rafters are spiked to the upper ends of the logs and the latter trimmed flush with the rafters. Then tack building paper to the logs above the nailing joist.

The height of the center pole determines the pitch of the roof. The roof shown in *Figures 2, 3,* and *9* rises 12 in. in 3 ft., a pitch that is about right for a cabin of this type and size. Note that the logs that support the purlins carry the weight of the ridge roof down to the foundation. These logs should be full length.

Now back to the fireplace again. The ridge pole and part of the frame will rest on the stonework as in *Figure 9*. The side wall of logs must be cut to fit closely to the masonry to make a weatherproof seal. A form for the flue can be made from a sheet of metal bent around two wood disks, the lower disk slightly smaller to give the form a taper, *Figure 11*. Wrap the form with paper so that it can be withdrawn from the concrete easily. After finishing the chimney to the ridge line allow it to set thoroughly before the ridge pole and the two purlins are put into place. These purlins will have to be trimmed to fit onto the supporting masonry. Both purlins and ridge should extend 2 ft.

over the walls to form wide eaves. With these parts in place the chimney can be finished to desired height.

Now for the interior logs. Begin with a narrow split log in a corner and make sure that the joint between the last log and the succeeding will fall on the flat face of the outside log in the same fashion as the "broken" joints in masonry or brick work, *Figure 1C.*

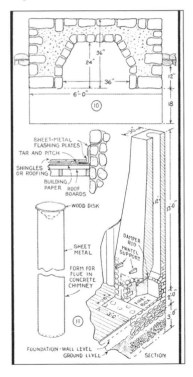

The roof: Before setting up the rafters, finish the gable ends with short logs. Center rafters can extend a few feet in front to provide a short roof overhang for a porch, *Figures 5* and *6.* Use ¾-in. stock for roof boards. A layer of building felt or paper goes on under the shingles. Flashing is built into the chimney in the manner shown in the upper detail, *Figure 11.*

Finishing the interior: *Figures 3* and *9* show how the doors, windows, and screens are installed and the trim put on.

After the top floor is laid, over building paper, the partitions are installed. Floor plans shown in *Figures 2, 4,* and *5* are suggested interior arrangements of rooms. Partitions are built up of split, peeled saplings that are nailed to each side of plywood sheets, *Figure 2.*

— BUILDING A YEAR-ROUND LOG CABIN —

You ou can build a log cabin of cedar, spruce, hemlock, tamarack, juniper, birch, poplar, hickory, oak, and pine. Hardwoods are satisfactory but difficult to handle. Bark improves the appearance but is subject to insects and borer infestation. When bark is left on the trees, they should be cut in the winter when the sap is down. Logs cut during warmer weather, when

ABOVE, LOGS HEWN WITH FLAT SIDES SO CORNER NOTCHING IS NOT NECESSARY. BELOW, CUT AND INTERLOCKING CORNER JOINTS THAT ARE RIGID.

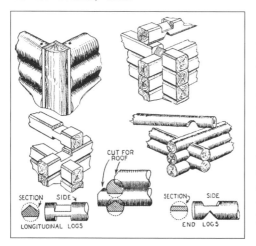

destructive insects are on the wing, should be painted or sprayed with a repellent. Bark can be removed readily when the sap is rising in the spring by girdling the tree or log every 4 ft. and making a vertical cut so that an ax blade can be slipped under the bark. Logs should have little or no taper and may vary from 6 to

10 in. in diameter at the small ends and should be 1 to 2 ft. longer than the side of the cabin, depending on the type of lock joint used at the corners.

For a permanent cabin, a concrete foundation is advisable. Holes, properly screened, should be provided for ventilation under the floor. The simplest footing for a temporary cabin consists of two large stones placed on compact ground to form each pier. A single rock in contact with the earth will "sweat," which in time will rot the wood. Or, a hole 3 ft. deep and 2 ft. in diameter is filled with small broken stones on which larger stones are placed. Wooden posts 10 to 12 in. in diameter, with the lower ends soaked in preservative and bedded on flat rocks, will also make good piers, although more durable piers can be built of masonry or concrete.

The strongest logs should be used for sills and first tiers. The sill should have its upper surface hewn flat and about 3 in. wide. The other logs should be hewn flat top and bottom so that they will lie close together. In laying the wall, the butts and tops should alternate to keep the wall level. Where the ends are not locked, and at every 9 ft. in the length of the wall, the top log should be fastened to the one under it by boring a 1½-in. hole through the upper one as well as through one-half of the thickness of the underlying one, and then driving in a hardwood pin.

TO PROTECT LOGS AGAINST DAMAGE FROM INSECTS, SPRAY WITH A PRESERVATIVE SOLUTION.

CAULKING WITH OAKUM, COTTON WASTE OR SPHAGNUM MOSS KEEPS CABIN COMFORTABLE BOTH SUMMER AND WINTER.

When the tops of the windows and doors are reached, the log just above these openings is cut out before laying the following tier. The openings may be cut later and the door and window frames installed. Floors of temporary cabins may be of clay and sand, packed hard. Puddle logs—logs laid on the ground with their top surfaces hewn flat—are also used for floors. Permanent cabins should have log or lumber floor joists. Joist logs, laid 2 or 3 ft. apart,

OLD BUGGY SPRING TO PEEL LOGS BEFORE CREOSOTING

to shed water quickly. The former is a slope of 22½ degrees, and the peak is one-half the length of the span above the plate. One-half pitch is a slope of 45 degrees, and the peak is one-half the length of the span above the plate. Poles from 4 to 6 in. in diameter are satisfactory for rafters. Roof sheathing is

should be about 6 in. in diameter for 12-ft. spans or less, 8 in. for 16-ft. spans, and about 9 in. for 20-ft. spans. The flooring for a 20-ft. span should be crowned 2 in. at the center to allow for subsequent sagging. Framing should be 2 in. from chimneys to prevent charring.

nailed over the rafters and shingles applied, doubling the first course at the eaves. Shingles should be laid 4½ in. to the weather on a ¼-pitch roof, and 5½ in. on a ½-pitch roof. One thousand shingles with a 5-in. exposure will cover 130 square feet. Ribs, valleys, and hips should be covered with 12-in. strips of tin or

The roof should be ¼ to ½-pitch

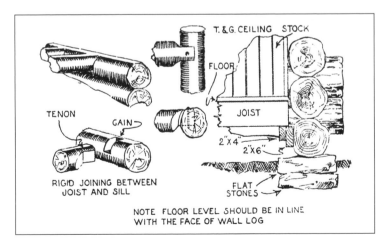

T. & G. CEILING STOCK

FLOOR

TENON

GAIN

JOIST

2"X4"

2"X6"

RIGID JOINING BETWEEN JOIST AND SILL

FLAT STONES

NOTE FLOOR LEVEL SHOULD BE IN LINE WITH THE FACE OF WALL LOG

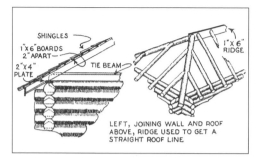

SHINGLES

1"x 6" BOARDS
2" APART

2"x 4"
PLATE

TIE BEAM

1" X 6"
RIDGE

LEFT, JOINING WALL AND ROOF
ABOVE, RIDGE USED TO GET A
STRAIGHT ROOF LINE

caulking iron and mallet. For the inside chinking, pieces of quarter round may be nailed into position. Or you may nail in strips of metal lath and fill up the crevices with cement mortar.

heavily tarred felt before laying shingles, and the chimney should be flashed.

The ridge consists of a 4-in. pole with a V-shaped groove or it may consist of two 6-in. saddle boards nailed together to form a V. A safe chimney is built of masonry with two or more flues with terra-cotta linings. It should be at least 20 ft. high so that it will draw well.

Cracks are chinked after the logs have dried out. If the logs have wide spaces between them, fill with slabs of stone bedded in clay. These are set at an angle of 45 or 60 degrees in lime or cement mortar. If the logs are laid close, the chinks are often caulked with cotton waste, oakum, or spaghnum moss formed into the joints from both sides of the log with a wooden wedge or

Where timber is not plentiful and the cost of building a log cabin would be a prohibitive factor, imitation log cabins can be built by using special siding. This is less trouble than felling trees, stripping off the bark, and hauling them to your site. The siding has a rounded face on one side and is nailed to studding as shown. In this method of construction, standard building practice is followed in setting up the framework and in laying the floor and roof. If you desire, the inside of the cabin may be finished with wall board.

LOG-CABIN EFFECTS WITH SPECIAL SIDING

— PERMANENT TENT COVERED WITH VINES —

You can make an attractive shelter that can hide a permanent tent in a campsite meant to be kept private, as shown in the drawing. It consists of a wooden frame covered with wire netting, over which vines are grown. The frame is made of seven 6-ft. two-by-fours, the rafters being set with their bases 5 ft. apart. These are then covered with wire netting, and the seeds of wild morning glory, clematis, or other rapidly growing vines are planted along the edges. The frame may be painted green for a better appearance. In six or eight weeks, the tent will be attractively camouflaged under the vines and will provide cool, pleasant shelter.

VINE-COVERED TENT IS PLEASING TO THE EYE AND HIDDEN IN DENSE GROWTH, MAKING FOR THE PERFECT PRIVATE CAMPSITE.

— CAMPS AND HOW TO BUILD THEM —

There are several ways of building a temporary camp from material that is always to be found in the woods. Whether these improvised shelters are intended to last until a permanent camp is built or only as a camp on a short excursion, a great deal of fun can be had in their construction. An evergreen tree with branches growing well down toward the ground furnishes all the material. By chopping the trunk almost through, so that when the tree falls the upper part will still remain attached to the stump, a serviceable shelter can be quickly provided. The cut should be about 5 ft. from the ground. Then the boughs and branches on the underside of the fallen top are chopped away and piled on top. There is room for several persons under this sort of shelter, which offers fairly good protection against any but the most drenching rains.

The wigwam sheds rain better, and where there are no suitable trees that can be cut, it is the easiest camp to make. Three long poles with the tops tied together and the lower ends spaced 8 to 10 ft. apart make the frame of the wigwam. Branches and brush can easily be piled up and woven in and out on these poles so as to shed a very heavy rain.

The brush camp is shaped like an ordinary "A" tent. The ridgepole should be about 8 ft. long and supported by crotched uprights about 6 ft. from the ground. Often the ridgepole can be laid from one small tree to another. Avoid tall trees on account of lightning. Eight or ten long poles are then laid slanting against the ridgepole on each side. Cedar or hemlock boughs make the best thatch for the brush camp. They should be piled up to a thickness of a foot or more over the slanting poles and woven in and out to keep them from slipping. Then a number of poles should be laid over them to prevent them from blowing away.

In woods where there is plenty of bark available in large slabs, the bark lean-to is a quickly constructed and serviceable camp. The ridgepole is set up like that of the brush camp. Three or four other poles are laid slanting to the ground on one side only. The ends of these poles should be pushed into the earth and fastened with crotched sticks. Long poles are then laid crossways of these slanting poles, and the whole can be covered with brush as in the case of the brush camp or with strips of bark laid overlapping each other like shingles. Where bark is used, nails are necessary to hold it in place. Bark may also be used for a wigwam, and it can be held in place by a cord wrapped tightly around the whole structure, running spiralwise from the ground to the peak. In the early summer, the bark can easily be removed from most trees by making two circular

The Wigwam

The Brush Camp

The Indian Camp

A Closed Lean-to, Thatched with Bark

Tongs

Broom of Hemlock Twigs

Packing Box Cupboard

Table and Chairs Combined

Stool Made of a Block

Bunk with Mattress of Springy Boughs

cuts around the trunk and joining them with another vertical cut. The bark is easily pried off with an ax, and if laid on the ground under heavy stones, will dry flat. Sheets of bark, 6 ft. long and 2 or 3 ft. wide, are a convenient size for camp construction.

The small boughs and twigs of hemlock, spruce, and cedar, piled 2 or 3 ft. deep and covered with blankets, make the best kind of a camp bed. For a permanent camp, a bunk can be made by laying small poles close together across two larger poles on a rude framework. Evergreen twigs or dried leaves are piled on this, and a blanket or a piece of canvas stretched across and fastened down to the poles at the sides. A bed like this is soft and springy and will last through an ordinary camping season. A portable cot that does not take up much room in the camp outfit is made of a piece of heavy canvas 40 in. wide and 6 ft. long. Four-inch hems are sewn in each side of the canvas, and when the camp is pitched, a 2-in. pole is run through each hem and the ends of the pole supported on crotch sticks.

Freshwater close at hand and shade for the middle of the day are two points that should always be looked for in a selecting a site for a camp. If the camp is to be occupied for any length of time, useful implements for many purposes can be made out of such material as the woods afford. The simplest way to build a crane for hanging kettles over the campfire is to drive two posts into the ground, each of them a foot or more from one end of the fire space, and split the tops with an ax so that a pole laid from one to the other across the fire will be securely held in the split. Tongs are very useful in camp. A piece of elm or hickory, 4 ft. long and 1½ in. thick, makes a good pair of tongs. For a foot in the middle of the stick, cut half of the thickness away and hold this part over the fire until it can be bent easily to bring the two ends together. Then fasten a crosspiece to hold the ends close together, shape the ends so that anything that drops into the fire can be seized by them, and a serviceable pair of tongs is the result. Any sort of a stick that is easily handled will serve as a poker. Hemlock twigs tied around one end of a stick make an excellent broom. Movable seats for a permanent camp are easily made by splitting a log, boring holes in the rounded side of the slab, and driving pegs into them to serve as legs. A short slab or plank can easily be made into a three-legged stool in the same way.

Campers usually have boxes in which their provisions have been carried. Such a packing box is easily made into a cupboard, and it is not difficult to improvise shelves, hinges, or a lock for the camp larder.

A good way to make a camp table is to set four posts into the ground and nail crosspieces to support slabs cut from chopped wood logs to form a top. Pieces can be nailed onto the legs of the table to hold other slabs to serve as seats, affording accommodation for several persons.

— HOMEMADE SHOULDER-PACK TENT —

After sleeping under various kinds of canvas coverings and not finding any of them entirely to my liking, I made the tent shown in the illustration, which proved quite satisfactory. It is of light weight, easily set up or taken down, and when buttoned closely is practically rain-, wind-, and bug-proof. The cost of materials necessary for making it is slight. I use it not only as a sleeping tent but also as a carryall in packing camping equipment. The canvas is supported by frames made of pliable branches cut in the woods.

The layout for the canvas is shown in the detailed drawings. The sections for the ends are made of three pieces, one for the ground and two, divided vertically, for the end covering. The ground section of the main portion of the tent and the covering are made in one piece, 6 ft.

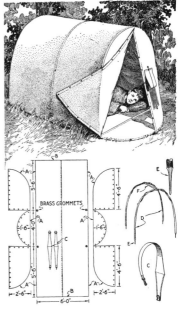

STAKES, ROPE BRACES, AND SUPPORTING POLES ARE NOT REQUIRED FOR THIS SHOULDER-PACK TENT, THE SUPPORTS BEING CUT AT THE CAMP.

wide, joined at the middle as shown. The adjoining edges A are sewn together and the edges B, which are set at the ridge of the tent, are sewn after the other pieces are joined. Brass grommets are fitted in the canvas, as indicated, and the points of the supporting frames pass through them in driving the supports into the ground. The shoulder straps C are placed so that they are in position when the tent is folded and rolled into a pack. Other equipment may be placed inside of it. The tent supports

D are pointed at the ends E and are twisted together at the top. The ridgepole F steadies them and holds the canvas at the middle.

To set up the tent, lay the canvas flat on the ground and place the supports, twisted together, through the grommets. Spring them into the ends of the canvas and insert the ridgepole by springing it between the supports. The canvas is 8-oz. duck, and the fastenings used are snap buttons; buttonholes, buckles, or harness snaps may also be used.

Mobile Home

— Hiker's Tepee Tent Folds into a Light Bundle for Carrying —

This novel tent was used several seasons by a woodsman. It is set up around a tree trunk, which serves as a center pole so that all the hiker carries is the canvas and the drawstring or top cord. The tent consists of several segments sewed together tepee fashion, with a ground diameter of 10 ft. and a center hole that can be opened to 10 in. A number of small rope loops are sewed to the lower edge, through which small

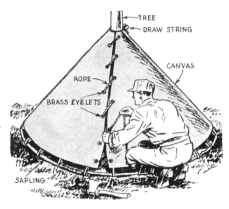

saplings are run and the ends lashed together to keep the canvas taut.

Building *a* Camp Car

— Chassis and Body Construction —

The camp car, or land cruiser, described here evolved from long experience in summer touring, and is the fruit of much thought and preliminary investigation.

Many plans were made, designs drawn up, checked over thoroughly, and then discarded, and much experimenting was done before the car was finally built. Since being constructed, the car has been driven over 5,000 miles, providing every satisfaction.

SIDE VIEW OF THE CAMP CAR READY FOR THE ROAD. THIS CAR HAS GIVEN EXCELLENT SERVICE IN TOURING.

Some of the considerations involved in the construction of a car of this type are the following: It must be light weight; everything must be contained under one roof—that is, there must be no sections extending beyond the protection of the roof, whether traveling or in camp; it must allow the driver good vision in every direction; it must afford comfort to all passengers when riding, and good beds when camping; it must have provision for carrying a supply of safe drinking water, and for the preparation of meals; it should have an ice box, and as many cupboards and lockers as possible. These provisions are only necessities, and were not at all hard to embody in the final design.

In designing the car, the body width was determined by the space necessary for the berths and seats. The builder desired that when carrying four passengers the seats should afford each a good view. The seats were accordingly to be individual, and were located in the car as shown in the floor plan; they are held in this position by cleats, but may be removed and used in any part of the car, as desired.

The length was the next consideration. After some figuring, the

FRONT VIEW, SHOWING THE CLEAR-VISION WINDSHIELD THAT ALLOWS EACH PASSENGER AN UNOBSTRUCTED VIEW.

builder decided to allow the body to overhang the rear axle by 5 ft., and the body was so built. After one season's use, however, the wheelbase was lengthened and the overhang reduced to 3 ft. It was possible to make the floor 12 ft. long. The headroom was determined by the builder's height, and this left only one main dimension to be determined—the length of the "snout," or overhanging part of the roof. It needed to house the berth that is swung over the hood in front of the steering wheel. The bed or berth was made 4 ft. wide, so as to take a regular mattress. This, then, fixed the amount of overhang.

The first tour taught much about chassis design and construction. The 5-ft. overhang was found to impose too much weight on the rear axle. Although this was all right as far as steering and traction for hard pulls were concerned, it did not make for a steady-riding car or good tire economy. The original wheelbase was 123 in. By moving the rear axle back 24 in., a much better balance was obtained, and the body design was unaltered, except as to floor arrangement. The present wheelbase is 147 in., and the weight on each wheel, with full load, is about 1,500 pounds.

The first touring-car frame being too light, it was discarded. Two lengths of 4-in. channel iron were used instead. A short connecting length of the same-size channel was welded across the front, to form a bumper and brace the frame, and another length across the frame, to carry the front end of the torque arm. The remaining cross members are either 1½-in. pipe or sections cut from the old frame. The frame was made narrow enough to allow the springs to be mounted on the outside.

The front springs are 40 in. long, and are mounted under the frame in the usual manner; each has nine leaves, 2 in. wide. The rear springs are 56 in. long, and have fourteen 2-in. leaves each. The rear ends of the springs are fitted with sliding contacts instead of shackles.

The first season, the rear springs were underslung, with long shackles at the rear. This, however, allowed the springs to twist and the car to sway badly. With the present construction there is no sideways movement, and riding comfort is all that can be desired. Four heavy snubbers are used to check rebound.

A full-floating type rear axle was taken from a heavy touring car. It has adjustable taper-roller bearings throughout. The gear ratio is 4½ to 1, but 5 to 1 would be better. The front axle is of the usual I-beam type, designed for touring-car service.

The 6-cylinder engine is of the standard L-head type, 3½-in. bore by 5-in. stroke, with a rating of 29½ hp. It is an engine designed for service in a passenger car weighing about 2,700 lbs. The transmission is standard. The engine is powerful enough to keep the car moving even in very bad going, although, in hard pulls, the 5-to-1 gear ratio in the rear axle would help considerably.

The speed in high gear ranges from about 5 to over 45 miles per hour. Although, of course, the average touring speed is around 30 miles per hour.

The tires and rims are worthy of more consideration than they usually receive. Nothing less than a 4½-in. truck cord, or a 5-in. passenger-car cord tire, should be used for a car of this weight. The rims should be one of the several types that make contact with the tire all the way around.

The foregoing information is given not so much with the idea that others will assemble a special chassis, as the builder did, but rather that the main points of this design are considered in selecting a chassis. There are a number of fast, light trucks on the market, among which a suitable

FIGURE 1: PLAN. FIGURE 2: SIDE ELEVATION OF ASSEMBLED CHASSIS FOR CAMP CAR. FIGURE 3: FLOOR PLAN, SHOWING LOCATION OF CHAIRS WHILE DRIVING, STOVE, ICE BOX, AND OTHER EQUIPMENT. FIGURE 4: DETAILS OF THE BODY FRAME, SHOWING WINDOW FRAMES IN PLACE, AND CONNECTION OF FRONT POSTS AND RAFTER TO TRUSS MEMBER.

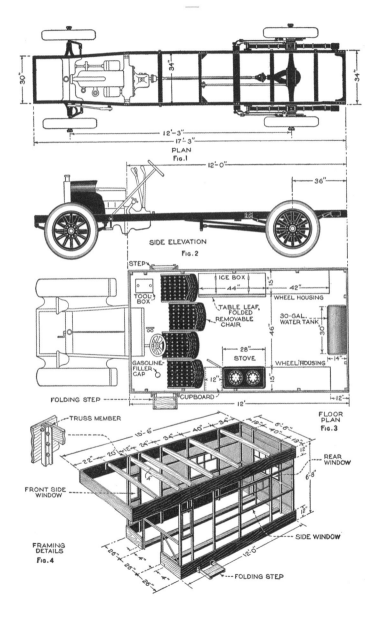

PLAN
Fig. 1

SIDE ELEVATION
Fig. 2

STEP

ICE BOX

TOOL-BOX

TABLE LEAF,
FOLDED
REMOVABLE
CHAIR

WHEEL HOUSING

30-GAL.
WATER TANK

STOVE

WHEEL HOUSING

GASOLINE-FILLER
CAP

CUPBOARD

FOLDING STEP

FLOOR
PLAN
Fig. 3

TRUSS MEMBER

REAR
WINDOW

FRONT SIDE
WINDOW

SIDE WINDOW

FRAMING
DETAILS
Fig. 4

FOLDING STEP

chassis may be found. If a touring-car chassis is used, it should be one with a very rigid frame, an engine of the specifications outlined above, and good springs. A suitable chassis will be more commonly found among the higher-priced cars than among the low- and medium-priced ones.

The chassis being ready, the framing of the body may proceed. The job will probably have to be modified to fit the chassis. But the dimensions given will be of material help and, in many cases, can be followed without change. When assembling, the builder should watch the road clearance; this should not be less than 10 to 12 in. If the body is to be framed on the chassis, it is wise to set the latter in such a position that it will not be disturbed while work is in progress, and to block it level. If this is not done, every deflection of the springs, or change in tire pressure, will throw the job out of level, and result in delay.

The sills used for the frame are 2-by-4 in. oak, although any good hardwood will answer. The manner of attaching the sills to the frame will vary. In a touring-car chassis with a hump in it to run over the rear axle, the sills may be set on edge, in such a manner that the front ends rest on the top of the side members of the frame. If the frame is straight on top, the sills may be laid flat, as shown in *Figure 4.* Another method is to bolt the sills to the side of the frame. A point to keep in mind is that every inch that the sills project above the frame means an inch added to the height of the body. This means much, not only in looks but in clearance on the sides and under bridges, etc. In laying the sills, the builder must also take care to see that they will clear other parts of the car as they move up and down with the spring action.

Having bolted the sills to the frame as seems best, the floor—of No. 1 common pine—is laid. Two boards are cut to the necessary length, one being fastened to the front end of the sills, the other to the rear, at right angles, determining the four corners of the lower part of the body. The rear board may have the groove sides planed down, and the edge laid even with the ends of the sills. It must be squared carefully with the front board and sills before being nailed down. The flooring comes next.

Wherever possible, the floorboards are laid full length; that is, clear across the width of the body. There are no cross sills, for two reasons. First, they raise the floor from 2 to 4 in. Second, they tend to make the frame more rigid, and more subject to racking on rough roads.

The position of the engine, transmission, and wheels will determine the location of the parts that must be cut out of the floor. The old floorboards may be used, but the builder will usually find it necessary to use new lumber.

As cross-sills are eliminated, other members must be used to take their place. The floor helps but cannot be depended on to do the work alone. At the front, any wood sill or truss would prove too bulky and insecure. Accordingly, the truss member, *Figure 5,* was evolved. This is made from 1¼-in. angle and T-iron. All joints are welded, and the rabbets formed are set to the front so that the windshield may have a proper set when closed. The two short center posts are bolted to the front ends of the sills and rest on a steel plate, fitted onto the top edges of the car frame. Two pieces of ¼ by 1-in. steel are welded into the outer panels, as shown, for braces. These prevent the outer edges of the body from sagging. The space between the long

posts is filled by the windshield while traveling, and by the forward berth while camping.

The side sills are pine or poplar, 2 by 2-in. in size, nailed under the edges of the floorboards, when the latter are cut to length. Pieces of the same material are used to bind the edges of the floor cut-outs. The rear edge of the floor is strengthened with a 2 by 2-in., or 1 by 4-in. sill, depending on the method of attaching the main sills to the car frame.

Having the truss member erected and all edges of the floor bound and strengthened, the next step is to lay out the studs, or posts.

The approximate position of the posts may be gathered from *Figures 3* and *4;* good, sound oak or ash, 1½ in. square, is used for these. The posts are half-lapped at the bottom, to the floor and 2-in. sills, and the joints fastened with screws, after coating the surfaces with paint to prevent penetration of moisture. As the posts are set they are plumbed, laths being used to brace them in position. The front posts are fastened to the truss angles with screws.

It will be noted, in *Figure 4,* that there is a 12-in. board bolted to the bottom and top of the posts on each side. These are poplar, known as panel stock by lumber dealers. The bottom boards are ¾ in. thick, and the top ones ½ in. thick. These boards take the place of heavy cross and longitudinal sills and are fastened to the posts with ⁵/₁₆-in. bolts. This construction ensures sufficient rigidity to prevent racking of the body, while permitting considerable twisting without damage. No corner or diagonal braces are used.

The rafters are of 1⅜-in. oak or ash; they are 2 in. wide at the ends, and 4 in. at the center. If additional headroom is desired, they may be cut out to a curve on the underside, starting the curve at a point 16 in. from each end, and making the height of the chord 1½ in. That is, the width at the center would be 2½ in. A rafter is set at each post, which results in uneven spacing, but is best for strength. One ⁵/₁₆-in. bolt is used to fasten the rafter, at each end, to the posts, which are notched ⅜ in. to take the ends of the rafters. In the overhanging end of the top, short posts are fastened to support the rafters.

Short pieces of the post material are used in the corners of the top as bolting pieces for the panel boards, and similar pieces along the edges as nailing cleats for the roof sheathing. The two rear side windows and the rear window are arranged to slide up for ventilation. When traveling at touring speed, however, there is a great amount of suction at the rear off the car, and the dust whipped up sifts in at every crevice. Becuase it is hard to make a sliding joint snug enough to exclude this dust, it may be best to make only the side windows slide. The posts are used as the side frames. The window sills are ½-in. stuff, set at a slight angle to ensure drainage. The window cap is merely a piece of quarter-round molding, nailed over the lattice strip that holds onto the duck covering. The window frames cannot be finished until the body has been covered.

The roof may be covered with the regular roof sheathing used by body makers or, as in the present case, with ⅜-in. oak flooring. The smooth side is laid to the rafters, because this forms the ceiling, and is stained and varnished. The sheathing is fastened

FIGURE 5: TRUSS FOR FRONT OF BODY. FIGURE 6: DETAILS OF ROOF COVERING AND LOCKER FRAMING. FIGURE 7: METHOD OF APPLYING DUCK COVERING TO SIDES AND REAR. FIGURE 8: DETAILS OF WINDOWS. FIGURE 9: ONE-HALF OF WINDSHIELD, SHOWING VENTILATING FRAME. FIGURE 10: DOOR CONSTRUCTION, SHOWING SLIDING WINDOW.

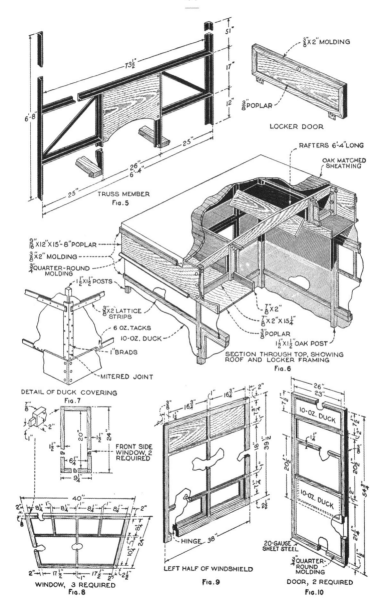

51"

⅜"X2" MOLDING

73½"

17"

12"

¾"POPLAR

LOCKER DOOR

6'-8"

RAFTERS 6'-4" LONG

OAK MATCHED
SHEATHING

25"

26"
6'-4"

25"

TRUSS MEMBER
Fig.5

⁹⁄₁₆"X12"X15'-8"POPLAR

⅜"X2" MOLDING

¾"QUARTER-ROUND
MOLDING

1½"X1½" POSTS

⅜"X2" LATTICE
STRIPS

6 OZ. TACKS

10-OZ. DUCK

1" BRADS

MITERED JOINT

DETAIL OF DUCK COVERING
Fig.7

⅞"X2"

⅜"X2"X15¼"

¾"POPLAR

1½"X1½"OAK POST

SECTION THROUGH TOP, SHOWING
ROOF AND LOCKER FRAMING
Fig.6

⅞"
2"

1"
2"

20"

1½"

1½"

24

6¼"

9¼"

FRONT SIDE
WINDOW, 2
REQUIRED

40"

2" 8¼" 8¼" 8¼" 8¼" 2"

24½"

10½"

2" 17½" 1" 17½" 2½" 2½"

WINDOW, 3 REQUIRED
Fig.8

⅜"

16¾" 16¾" 1" 16¾" 2"

39½"

16"

2½"

HINGE 38"

LEFT HALF OF WINDSHIELD
Fig.9

26"

23"

7½"

10-OZ. DUCK

1½"

1¼"

20½"

20½"

10-OZ. DUCK

54¾"

2¼"

20-GAUGE
SHEET STEEL

¾"QUARTER-
ROUND
MOLDING

DOOR, 2 REQUIRED
Fig.10

with 1-in. flathead nails, well punched down. With the framing finished as in *Figure 4,* and the roof sheathing on, the duck roof covering is applied.

This may be obtained from a body-trimmer's supply house, in a width sufficient to cover

the roof without a seam. The corners of the sheathing should be rounded to prevent cutting the covering. Each edge of the covering is drawn down to a line on the panel board 3 in. from the top of the sheathing and tacked fast. The edges are then trimmed, if necessary, and covered with a ⅜ by 2-in. lattice strip. These details are clearly shown in *Figure 6.*

Before covering the sides, the posts are braced on the inside by means of lattice strips tacked to the centers to prevent them from being pulled out of line as the material is stretched. One edge of the side covering is tacked to the rear door post, and the duck is run back to the rear edge, making no allowance for the window opening. It is best to cut the material at the rear corner, putting

on only one side at a time. Don't attempt to run around the rear and up the other side without cutting. Note, in *Figure 7,* that the duck is fastened between panel board and posts, at top and bottom. The nuts are slacked, the material tucked in, and the bolts drawn tight again. This avoids cutting the material.

With the top and bottom tacked in place, the lattice strips are applied. These are ⅜- by 2-in. molding strips. A strip is nailed on the outside of the duck so that it will just touch the bottom of the window sills when these are in place. A second strip is nailed 23 in. above this, to form part of the window cap. These strips run from the rear door post to the rear corner post on each side, and across the rear, in like manner. The strips do not meet at the corners but are cut short to allow room for the vertical strips that cover the tacks fastening the duck to the corner posts. When fastening the vertical lattice strips at the window posts, they are allowed to project over the posts about ⅜ in., to form shoulders against which the windows rest and slide.

The temporary lattice strips tacked on the inside are now removed and strips, long enough to reach between the posts, are fastened on the inside of the duck by nailing to the outside strips. A helper, holding a heavy sledge or dolly against the strips, is necessary for this part of the job. Flathead nails, ¾ in. long, are used for this, heads inside, where they do not spoil the appearance of the job. No inside strips are placed above the windows because they would interfere with raising the latter.

After the sides are finished, the window openings are cut out, and the body forward of the doors is covered and paneled to conform to the rear. The front side-window frames are fastened to the posts, and the duck tacked to them.

The windows, shown in *Figure 8,* have frames of poplar or pine, rabbeted ¼ in. wide and ½ in. deep to receive the glass. The glass is retained in the rabbets by ¼-in. square molding. All joints are mortise-and-tenon, and the panes may be arranged in any manner desired.

The windshield, the left half of which is shown in *Figure 9,* is set in the upper part of the truss member. Each side is framed to fill half of the opening in the truss, the full width being 6 ft. 4 in. The halves are joined at the center by a ⅜-in. rabbet. Aside from filling the opening properly, when used as a windshield these parts also form the sides of the housing for the upper berth when they are lowered. They carry part of the weight of the bed when raised. Therefore, the frame is made of hardwood.

When opened, the top edges overlap the panel boards 1 in., which prevents the windows from opening too far and makes them weatherproof. Mortise-and-tenon joints are used throughout, and the glass panes are fastened in the same manner as in the side windows. The lower panels are filled in with light oak frames, carrying two panes of glass each. The frames are hinged at the bottom and may be dropped for ventilation. When up, they are held in position by metal thumb buttons.

The halves are hinged to the truss posts and clear the web of the T-iron top rail by 3/16 in. Three hinges are used on each side. In framing, the builder must bear in mind that the frames are right- and left-hand, or they will not mate when hung.

The door frames, *Figure 10*, are made of hardwood. Each door is provided with a sliding window that drops into a pocket—much like a sedan window. Double-strength glass is used, in a light wood frame. Duck is used to cover the top and bottom of the door. This is tacked, on the inside, in the rabbet provided for the window frame. Where this does not run, strips of quarter-round molding are used. Edges where molding is not used are rounded with a rasp, so that all exposed edges are round. Corner joints are half-lapped and screwed, and cross rails tenoned into mortises in the side-pieces. The window frame is held in by means of a 20-gauge sheet metal pocket, and by lattice strips screwed to the frame.

Three carriage hinges are used on each door along with deck locks, with a permanent handle fitted. The sheet metal forming the pocket should be painted body steel or galvanized. It is so formed that any water blowing in at the window joint will run out over the flange at the bottom off the door. The edges of the doors are made snug by trimming them with aluminum T-molding, purchased from a body-builder's supply house. The windows are raised or lowered by straps attached to the frame and are held closed by small "triggers" that swing under the frame.

— INTERIOR FITTINGS —

Having built and covered the frame, the berths and other interior fittings may be constructed.

At the front of the car, in *Figure 11*, will be a duck-covered frame; this serves several purposes. When the car is closed up ready for traveling, the back end of the frame rests on the top of the windshield, as shown in *Figure 13*. This protects the berth

FIGURE 11: VIEW OF LEFT AND FRONT INTERIOR, SHOWING LOCATION OF UTENSIL AND SUPPLY CUPBOARDS, GASOLINE STOVE, AND FRONT BERTH. FIGURE 12: VIEW OF RIGHT REAR END, SHOWING LOCKERS, REAR BERTH, AND REFRIGERATOR. FIGURE 13: DETAILS OF FRONT-BERTH ARRANGE-MENT. FIGURE 14: WORKING DRAWING OF FRONT BERTH.

45

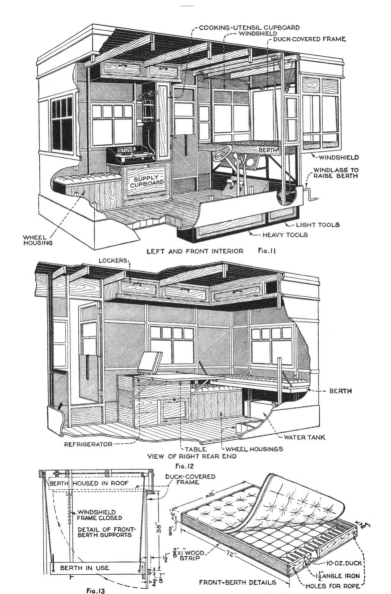

COOKING-UTENSIL CUPBOARD
WINDSHIELD
DUCK-COVERED FRAME

BERTH

WINDSHIELD

WINDLASS TO
RAISE BERTH

STOVE

SUPPLY
CUPBOARD

LIGHT TOOLS
HEAVY TOOLS

WHEEL
HOUSING

LEFT AND FRONT INTERIOR   Fig. 11

LOCKERS

BERTH

WATER TANK

REFRIGERATOR

TABLE   WHEEL HOUSINGS
VIEW OF RIGHT REAR END
Fig. 12

BERTH HOUSED IN ROOF

DUCK-COVERED
FRAME

WINDSHIELD
FRAME CLOSED

DETAIL OF FRONT-
BERTH SUPPORTS

38"

BERTH IN USE

Fig. 13

¾"X1" WOOD
STRIP

72"

10-OZ. DUCK

1½" ANGLE IRON

HOLES FOR ROPE

FRONT-BERTH DETAILS

Fig. 14

from dust and dirt. When the berth is down, the frame forms the front wall of the sleeping recess. The frame is made of 1 by 4-in. poplar, and is hinged to a stout cleat in the "nose" of the car. The hinges are firmly bolted to both frame and cleat, because they carry part of the weight of the berth and its occupants. The immediate point that receives the weight of the berth is a cleat running across the frame, as shown in section in *Figure 13*. To keep the berth from slipping from this cleat, two iron brackets, shown dotted, are screwed to it and fit behind the berth frame. Most of the weight of the berth is carried by the cross member of the truss, shown in *Figure 13,* just below the windshield.

The duck used to cover the frame need not run below the cleat just mentioned. The side rails project below this, and form convenient handles for lifting the frame. A grooved rail on the front of the frame fits over the top of the windshield when the car is closed.

The front berth, shown in *Figure 14,* is made from a discarded bedspring, the end angle irons of the bed being screwed or bolted to the endpieces of a 48 by 72-in. wooden frame. The endpieces of the frame

cover the ends of the sidepieces, to prevent trouble due to the pull of the springs. The bottom of the berth is covered with duck, which may be paneled with lattice strips if desired.

The windlass-and-pulley arrangement for raising the berth is shown in *Figures 11* and *13.* The pulleys are placed so that the small ropes running to the corners of the berth may be attached to a larger rope, which is run to the windlass. The latter is a length of ½-in. pipe, mounted in wooden blocks on the frame, and provided with a gear and dog for a ratchet. The pipe projects through the front panel board, and a crank, fitted with a pin that engages slots cut in the pipe, is used to turn it. The crank is stored in the car when not in use. The gear is pinned to the pipe just inside the front post, and the pawl is fastened to the post so that it will prevent the gear from turning backward, except when the pawl is raised. The ropes used at the four corners are medium-weight sash cord; the windlass rope is of the same type, but heavier.

The rear berth, shown installed in *Figure 12* and in detail in *Figure 15,* is made from a so-called sanitary couch. All parts are discarded except those that can be used to make up the two light 2 by 6-ft. frames. After the frame pieces are cut to size they are welded together, although riveting will serve just as well. The springs are then fitted into each section, and the frames fastened together by means of four hinges, as shown in the detail. Two other heavy strap hinges were fastened to the berth and to the rear posts, as indicated, and hooks and studs fitted to secure the two parts together when folded against the wall, or when used at half width. The method of folding is shown in the upper detail. The half mattresses used are fastened to the frames by means of heavy cord. Two heavy chains, attached to the side posts, support the front of the berth, while allowing it to be doubled up when traveling.

The ceiling lockers are shown in *Figures 11* and *12*. There are five of these, two at each side and one across the rear. The rear one is 12 in. wide, 3 ft. deep, and 6 ft. long, and easily contains all the spare bedding. The side locks are not so large, and are used for clothing and other articles in constant use. The method of framing the lockers is clearly shown in *Figure 6*. Each door is cut from a single piece of ⅜-in. lumber, and the edges are bound with lattice strips.

This makes a neat but light door. Thumb buttons or catches are used on the ends of each door to prevent rattling.

The combined refrigerator and table, *Figure 16*, is made throughout of ⅜-in. soft wood. Wide boards were used to minimize the number of joints necessary. The entire box, with the exception of the small cupboard, is made with a double skin, ⅜-in. strips being used to separate the boards. The lids are of the same type of construction; this ensures fairly good insulation. The ice is set in through the large top door and rests on a slatted frame at the bottom, just over the drain. The ice compartment is lined with galvanized iron and the drain pipe is run through the floor. A sliding shelf or rack (not shown) is also fitted in this compartment. The small cupboard is built with but a single thickness of lumber and has no connection to the main compartment.

A table leaf is hinged to the front of the box, supported by two ⅛ by 1-in. steel braces. The leaf itself is made from a single piece of ⅜-in. poplar, 16 in. wide, and is strengthened by three cleats.

The supply cupboard, shown in *Figure 17*, is also made of ⅜-in. stock.

All except the top and shelves, which are made from flooring boards, to ensure strength. The construction is clearly shown in the drawing.

The cooking-utensil cupboard is built to fit the space between the supply cupboard and one of the overhead lockers. Its position is shown in *Figure 11,* and its construction in *Figure 18.*

The gasoline stove is mounted on the supply cupboard as shown in *Figure 11.* This is the standard type used for home cooking, but several inches are cut from the bottom and all joints carefully riveted. A vacuum tank is used instead of the reservoir originally furnished. Connection from this tank to the stove is made with 5/16-in. copper tubing. The supply line is connected to the rear gasoline tank, which is filled with high-test gasoline. A small vacuum pump is connected to the vacuum line at the top of the tank, and a few strokes of this will fill the tank with gasoline, so that no fuel is ever handled in open vessels to supply the stove.

The water tank, *Figure 12,* has a

30-gal. capacity and is set on the floor at the rear of the car. A ¾-in. pipe is run, under the floor, to the rear of the car, where it is fitted with a tee. The side outlet is fitted with a 16-in. length of pipe, the upper end being capped. This is the filler pipe. The other opening in the tee is fitted with a regular faucet. Filling the tank and drawing water are done outside the car. This tank may be made by anyone handy at sheet-metal work. It is made of 20-gauge galvanized iron and is fitted with a center baffle plate to prevent splashing. A pressure system, tried at first, proved to be too troublesome.

The tool box, *Figure 19,* is made of 20-gauge auto body steel over a wood frame. The rear compartment, carrying spades, chains, rope, jack, etc., is reached from the outside. The front compartment, carrying small tools, is reached through a trapdoor in the car floor. In framing this box, the builder should remember that it is to be swung under the floor, and make the frame accordingly.

Four chairs are provided, one of which is shown in *Figure 20.* They

FIGURE 15: DETAILS OF REAR BERTH. FIGURE 16: CONSTRUCTION OF REFRIGERATOR AND TABLE. FIGURES 17 AND 18: SUPPLY AND COOKING-UTENSIL CUPBOARD DETAILS. FIGURE 19: METHOD OF MAKING TOOLBOX. FIGURE 20: FRAMING AND UPHOLSTERING OF CHAIR, SHOWING METHOD OF FASTENING CHAIR TO FLOOR.

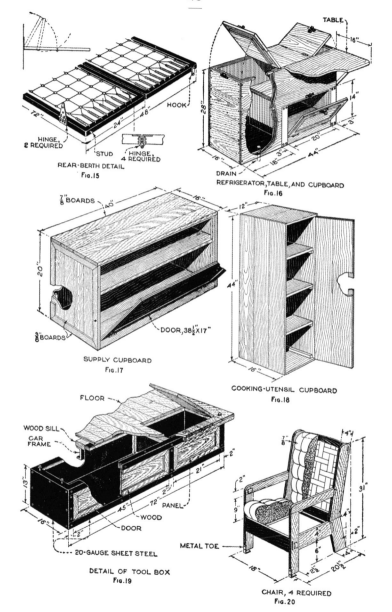

TABLE

HOOK

HINGE, 2 REQUIRED

STUD   HINGE, 4 REQUIRED

REAR-BERTH DETAIL
Fig. 15

72"   24"   48"

DRAIN

28"   14"

18"   3"   20"   3"

44"

REFRIGERATOR, TABLE, AND CUPBOARD
Fig. 16

7/8" BOARDS   40"   16"

20"

7/8" BOARDS

DOOR, 38½"×17"

SUPPLY CUPBOARD
Fig. 17

12"

44"

16"

COOKING-UTENSIL CUPBOARD
Fig. 18

FLOOR

WOOD SILL
CAR FRAME

13"   16"   2"   45"   72"   21"   2"

PANEL

WOOD

DOOR

20-GAUGE SHEET STEEL

DETAIL OF TOOL BOX
Fig. 19

METAL TOE

7/8"   4"   31"   9"   4"   2"   6"   18"   2½"   20½"

CHAIR, 4 REQUIRED
Fig. 20

LEFT, CAR COMPLETE, READY FOR THE ROAD, WITH BERTH HOUSED AND WINDSHIELD IN PLACE. RIGHT, WINDSHIELD OPEN, BERTH DOWN, AND DUCK-COVERED FRAME IN POSITION FOR SLEEPING.

may be moved to any position desired, but to keep the driver's seat in position while traveling, as shown in the floor plan, it is furnished with metal toes on the front legs. These slip under staples or metal cleats on the floor and make the seat quite secure. When the parts are framed and glued together, the webbing is nailed to the back. A small spring is then sewed on at each point where the webs cross. The springs are then tied in the usual manner, covered with burlap, the back padded with

cotton batting or hair and covered with material taken from an old touring-car seat, which can be secured at any car-wrecking house. It is also possible to cut sections of padding complete from old car-seat backs and tack them in place. Although this demands care, it is easier than building up the upholstery from the bottom.

The seat cushions may be made in a similar manner, from old touring-car seat cushions, the upholstering material being first removed from the springs. A frame is then prepared that will fit loosely into the chair frame and the old springs are fitted into this, wired, and tied in place, and the upholstering replaced.

The wheel housings must be made very tight and mounted snugly to the frame to exclude dirt. They are made of 20-gauge metal, wood-covered if desired, and all joints should be seamed, crimped, and riveted. Felt strips are used in the floor and side joints, coated with gasket cement, and screws used to draw the housings tight. The metal housings are quite strong enough to serve as seats, and cushions can be fitted to them. Dimensions cannot be given that will suit all cars, but the housings shown are 13 by 15 by 42 in.

Two gasoline tanks are carried, both mounted under the floor, outside the chassis frame at the left front corner. The forward tank is used almost exclusively for the engine, although both are connected so that either may be used if desired. The rear tank carries enough high-test gasoline for a month's cooking, and is connected to the stove as previously described. Both tanks have a 15-gal. capacity.

The construction of the remaining few fittings, such as the instrument board, folding steps, etc., can be gathered easily from the drawings. Many other fittings could be described, but because the necessity for these varies with the builder, they will be omitted. The painting and finishing, which is a matter of individual taste, need not be entered into here.

— CAR-TOP RACKS FOR CAMPERS —

If you are planning a camping trip this summer, whether it be just a day or two, or of long duration, one of these car-top racks will enable you to carry luggage or a boat with ease. The luggage rack shown in *Figure 1* has a large capacity and is attached securely to the car, yet is taken off easily by removing six screws. *Figure 2* shows the general assembly of the rack. Sides and ends are of wood, and the bottom consists of strips of flat iron and wire. Rubber at the crossing points of the strips and around the lower edges of the ends and sides protect the car top. The rack is attached to the gutters at six points above the doors and windows.

Those who take frequent short trips and want a boat rack that is

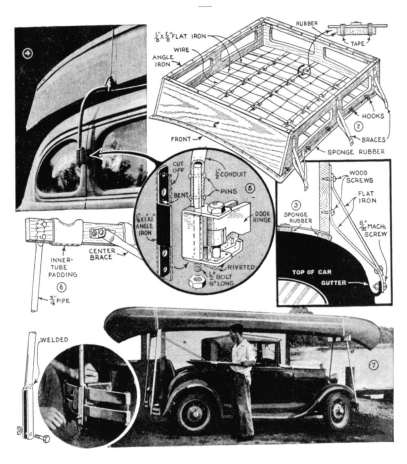

removed and replaced in a few minutes, will find the one in *Figure 4* just the thing. It consists of two lengths of pipe or conduit arched over the car top and fastened to the upper hinges off the four doors by means

of special brackets as shown in *Figure 5*. Each bracket is attached with a bolt, which is substituted for the hinge pin and riveted in place. Being small, the bracket remains on the car and is painted to match it.

Owners of coupes will find that the canoe rack in *Figure 7* solves their problem of carrying a boat above a short length top. The rack clamps to the bumpers, and a center brace from the rear support to the seat back takes care of end movement. Pipe is used for the supports.

FOREST FURNISHINGS

— ROUGH, RUGGED, AND RUSTIC CHAIRS, BENCHES, AND TABLES —

With the simple ruggedness of the tree trunks and branches from which it is made, rustic furniture is appropriate for campsite, porch, or cottage, and will withstand the weather indefinitely. Additional protection can be provided by applying spar varnish not only over the raw wood but also over the bark to prevent moisture from seeping between it and the wood. Because green wood shrinks considerably, which results in loosening of the

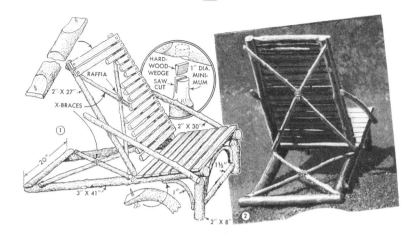

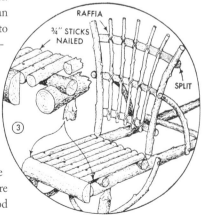

joints, only seasoned wood should be used except where sticks or branches are to be bent. These should be curved around a form and left to season for a few weeks in a warm, dry place such as the furnace room in winter or a sunny spot in summer. Also, it's better to use screws than nails because screws are less likely to loosen and pull out. This is especially true in regard to slats used as seats and backs where constant flexing of the slats tends to loosen nails.

Figure 1 shows a chair of easy but substantial construction. Two short legs are mortised into saplings that form the seat frame and serve as a rear support. To assure rigidity and tight joints, hardwood wedges are inserted into saw cuts in the tenons—as shown in the circular detail—to spread the tenons when they are forced into holes drilled in the frame. After the legs have been mortised, nails or screws can be

driven through the frame and into the tenons. Seat and back are split saplings flattened at the ends to fit snugly on the frame where they are screwed in place. To provide concave surfaces for greater comfort, these pieces may be shaped with a drawknife before fastening in place, and left slightly roughened rather than plane-smooth for rustic effect. Two X-braces, shown in *Figure 2,* are used as reinforcements to prevent twisting. These are bound with raffia, rawhide, or stout cord at the intersections, and are screwed to the frame. Arms, which serve as additional supports for the back, are fastened with countersunk screws concealed with plugs.

A similar chair is shown in *Figure 3.* Saplings form the frame and, as in the chair shown in *Figure 1,* two legs are attached by wedge-spread tenons and reinforced by curved braces on sides and front. Sticks forming the

seat are nailed to cross members that fit notches in the frame, and split molding covers the ends. On this chair, arms are omitted, a brace being substituted on each side to support a fan-shaped back. This is made of narrow pieces bound with raffia or stout cord to cross members screwed on curved uprights. The chair shown in *Figure 11* has willow whips for the seat and back to provide resiliency. Net sizes of all parts are shown in the cross-hatched drawing, *Figure 10.* Ends of the stretchers are cut concave to fit the round contour of the legs against which they are butted and screwed, as shown in the detail of *Figure 11.* A diagonal brace, attached to front and rear legs, wedges a center rail securely for attachment of willow whips. These are nailed to inside surfaces of the frame as indicated in the circular detail.

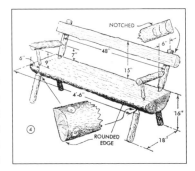

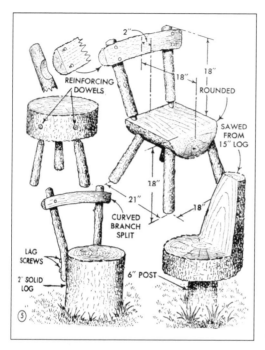

2"

REINFORCING DOWELS

18"

18"

ROUNDED

SAWED FROM 15" LOG

18"

21"

CURVED BRANCH SPLIT

18"

LAG SCREWS

2" SOLID LOG

6" POST

⑤

For the settee, *Figure 4,* a large split log about 9 or 10 in. in diameter is rounded at the edge and smoothed for a seat. Legs are set tightly in holes drilled at the desired angle in the underside, and secured with screws driven into counter-bored holes, which are plugged. Curved braces may be added for additional support if desired. A back rest is notched as shown and screwed to upright supports, which are drilled for

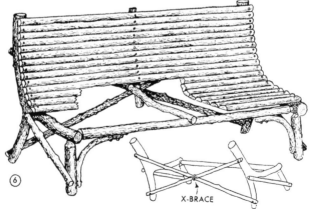

⑥

X-BRACE

tenons on the arms. For variation, the back and arms may be omitted to make a bench.

Chairs and stools to match the settee are shown in *Figure 5*. On the four-legged chair, the back rest is set into notches in the uprights, but the same construction may be followed as for the settee. If wood used for the

three-legged stool has a tendency to split easily when dry, ½-in. wooden dowels may be inserted in holes drilled across the grain and secured with waterproof glue. The two chairs or stools shown at the bottom of *Figure 5* illustrate what can be done with conveniently situated tree stumps. Edges of seats should be rounded to prevent snagging clothes.

Another settee can be made as illustrated in *Figure 6*. Crotched limbs, as nearly alike as possible, are cut for back supports and rear legs, and set aside to season. When the wood is thoroughly dried, holes are drilled for front legs, which are secured by wedges and screws as suggested for the chair shown in *Figure 1*, and a suitable piece is inserted to form a front rail. Curved braces are screwed to front

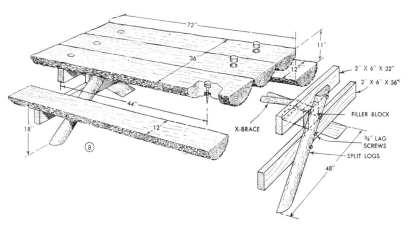

legs and rail, and an X-brace is attached as shown in the detail. Before the seat slats are nailed on, holes should be drilled for the nails to prevent splitting the dried frame.

Split-log slabs are excellent for a fixed outdoor table that will survive years of hard use. Large posts, well coated with preservative to prevent decay, are sunk into the ground below the frost line so that they will not heave. They are slotted as shown in *Figure 7* to take 2 by 6-in. crosspieces, which support half logs that form the top. Shallow logs or slabs are best for this purpose, and should be sawed or planed straight on each edge to fit together closely. Screws driven through the slabs into the crosspieces should be countersunk and plugged so as not be noticeable.

A similar table with built-on benches is shown in *Figure 8*. The crosspieces that support the table

and benches are mounted on split-log legs with a filler block secured at the intersection by a bolt. An X-brace consisting of 3-in. saplings is screwed to the crosspieces as shown in the photograph, *Figure 9*.

Another table, of lighter construction, is shown in *Figure 12*. Because finished lumber is used for the top, this table is suitable for indoor use in cottages and camps. Legs are glued into holes drilled in a 1 by 3-in. frame. Then the top is screwed to the frame. Holes for screws are counterbored and plugged, and bark-covered, split pieces are nailed along the edge for molding. Curved braces support legs and frame, and four short spreaders join the stretchers.

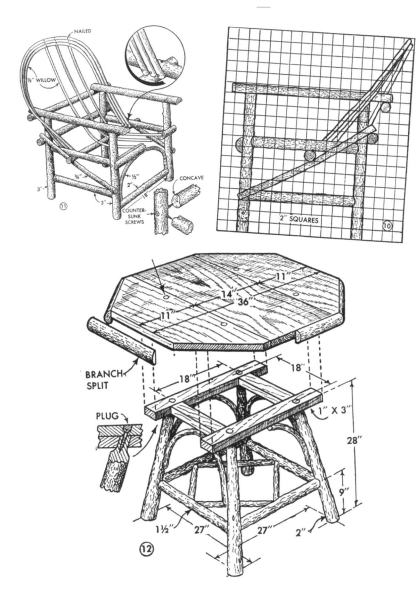

NAILED

½" WILLOW

CONCAVE

¾"
½"
2"
3"
3"

COUNTER-SUNK SCREWS

⑪

2" SQUARES

⑩

11"
14"
36"
11"

BRANCH SPLIT

PLUG

18"
18"

1" X 3"

28"

9"

1½"   27"   27"   2"

⑫

— A HAMMOCK ON WHEELS —

Because it is fitted with two wooden wheels at one end, you can push this hammock anywhere in wheelbarrow fashion. Cutouts at the foot end of the frame serve the purpose of handles for wheeling besides providing a means of adjusting the tension on the canvas. Uniformly molded edges, created with a shaper, give the job a neat, finished appearance. The two main side rails are each

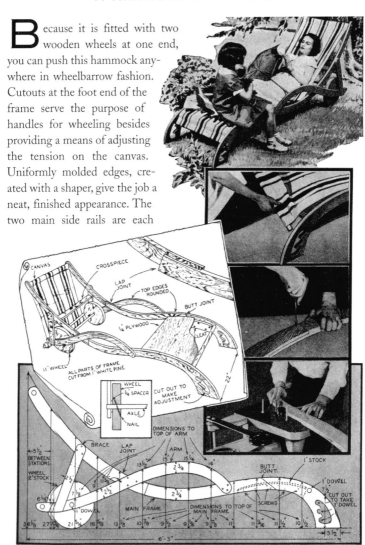

made up of three separate pieces, the upper-end center ones being half-lapped, while the center and lower ones are merely butt-joined on a cleat, which carries a plywood panel. All joints are glued and screwed.

— How to Make a Rustic Seat —

The rustic settee illustrated in *Figure 1* may be made 6 ft. long, which will accommodate four average-sized persons. It is not advisable to exceed this length, because it would then look out of proportion. Select the material for the posts, preferably branches that are slightly curved, as shown in the sketch. The front posts are about 3 ½ in. in diameter by 2 ft. 4 in. long. The back posts are 3 ft. 4 in. high, while the center post is 3 ft. 8 in. in height. The longitudinal and transverse rails are about 3 in. in diameter and their ends are pared away to fit the post to which they are connected by 1-in. diameter dowels. This method is shown in *Figure 4*. The dowel holes are bored at a distance of 1 ft. 2½ in., up from the lower ends of posts. The front center leg is partially halved to the front rail and also connected to the back post by a bearer, 4 in. deep

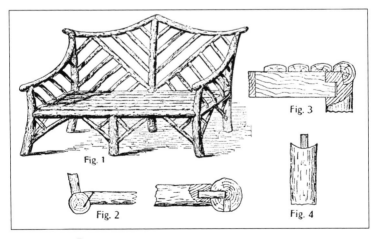

Fig. 1
Fig. 2
Fig. 3
Fig. 4

RUSTIC SEAT AND DETAILS OF CONSTRUCTION.

by 1½ in. thick. This bearer is tenoned to the back post.

Figure 3 shows a sectional view of the bearer joint to front leg, and also the half-round seat battens resting on the bearer, also showing them with their edges planed. It is wise to leave a space between the edges of each batten, say about ⅛ in., to allow rainwater to drain. The ends of the seat battens are pared away to fit the transverse rails neatly as shown in *Figure 2*. The struts for the post range in diameter from 1½ in. to 2 in. The ends of the struts are pared to fit the posts and rails, and are then secured with two or three brads at each end.

Select curved pieces, about 2½ in. in diameter, for the arm rests and back rails; while the diagonally placed filling may be about 2 in. in diameter. Start with the shortest lengths, cutting them longer than required, as the paring necessary to fit them to the rails and posts shortens them a little. Brad them in position as they are fitted, and try to arrange them at regular intervals.

— FOLDING SAWBUCK REQUIRES VERY LITTLE STORAGE —

Every camper finds it handy to have a sawbuck for occasional use when cutting up scrap wood, tree limbs, etc., for kindling, but many campers forgo this convenience because a sawbuck of the regular type requires so much storage space. However, one that folds will solve the problem. It is made in the usual way except that the two parts of each X-member are pivoted together with a bolt, and a chain is substituted for the usual bottom brace. This permits the sawbuck to fold flat so that it takes practically no storage space.

— THREE COTS MADE OUT OF TWO —

Two folding army cots are about all the average automobile tourist or camper wants to carry along with him, but if there are three members in the party, some sleeping arrangements must be provided for the "crowd."

The photograph shows how a party of three automobile tourists slept on two cots. Two sticks, the length of the cots when opened, were inserted through hems sewed into the sides of a strip of canvas to form a bed for the third person. This arrangement was slung between the two cots by means of straps, one end of which was fastened to the sticks, the free ends being passed around the side rails of the cots and buttoned on fasteners such as those used for fastening buggy curtains. Shorter sticks, notched at the ends, were inserted between the side sticks at the head and foot, below the canvas, to keep it stretched tight. The only objection to such a bed is that the person occupying the central part must wait until the other two members of the party have retired. Also, should one of the "outsiders" get up during the night or roll out of bed, the man in the center will be dropped down unless both cots are prevented from tipping over by driving a stake at each end and fastening the outside corners down with a short length of rope.

REDUCING THE BULK AND WEIGHT OF THE
CAMPER'S EQUIPMENT BY TAKING ONLY
TWO FOLDING COTS FOR THREE PERSONS—
THE THIRD SLEEPS ON A CANVAS STRIP
SLUNG BETWEEN THE TWO COTS.

In-Tents Concentration

— Keeping Rain Out of Tent —

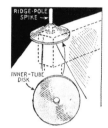

During long steady rains, water sometimes enters the ridge-pole openings of a tent. To avoid this, cut disks from an inner tube and impale them on the steel spikes that project through the holes.

A Dry Spot on a Rainy Day —

It often occurs when eating in a meadow by camp that a little rain shower spoils the day, even if it does no more than soak the grass and prevent the party from sitting down on it. The shower need not, however, affect the picnic at all if a piece of heavy canvas is suspended between the trees in the manner illustrated, so that a sort of shelter is provided, under which the grass remains perfectly dry.

The canvas can be of any desirable size and can be conveniently folded up and placed under the back seat of an auto. A brass eyelet is provided at each corner, to take the strain of the rope.

A PIECE OF CANVAS, TIED TO TREES, PROVIDES SHELTER FOR A PICNIC PARTY DURING A SHOWER

— HEATING INTERIOR OF TENT —

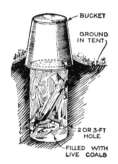

Heating the interior of a tent on a chilly night, or when clothes are to be dried, is usually a matter of considerable difficulty when a stove is unavailable. It is out of the question to light an open fire, because the smoke would be intolerable.

A large metal can or pail is inverted on the ground inside the tent, and a mark made around the edge. Inside this circle a hole, 2 or 3 ft. deep, is made. This hole is filled with live coals from an outside fire, and the bucket or can is pressed down over the top. Earth may be piled around the edge to make it absolutely smoke-tight. In a short time the tent will be comfortably warm, and the bucket will continue to radiate heat for hours with no danger from fire and smoke.

— AN IMPROVED TENT PEG —

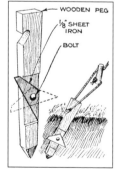

Many different ideas have been applied to making a tent peg that will not pull out of the ground, but the one illustrated has the merit of using cheap and easily obtained wooden pegs with a simple attachment that prevents them from being pulled out by accident.

A mortise is cut on one side of the peg to accommodate a triangular piece of sheet iron, pivoted to swing freely. The pegs are driven in the usual manner, but when any undue strain is placed on the tent ropes, the sheet-iron piece assumes the position indicated by the dotted lines and locks it as securely as the character of the soil will permit.

— SECURING TENT PEGS IN DAMP EARTH —

To keep tent stakes from pulling out of the ground during damp weather, drive them in at the same angle as the tent ropes to which they are attached. The experience of many campers has been that this is more effective than placing the pegs in the usual way.

— PROTECTORS FOR IRON TENT STAKES —

Iron stakes have been generally adopted by auto campers. The form made from light channel iron is widely used, but it has one disadvantage: The top soon becomes battered, making the edges so sharp that they are dangerous. During a camping trip last summer, one of the family's children who was barefoot, stepped on a stake and was injured. A short time later, one of the grown folks had a sandal torn by coming in contact with a stake. As a result of these experiences, the campers determined to provide some sort of

protectors. After some search for the proper thing, the idea of using short pieces of ¾-in. garden hose was suggested and tried. Each one was 2¾ in. long and a ½ by 1¼-in. hole was cut in the side. This rubber guard is slipped over the top of the stake after is has been driven in.

— WALL POCKETS IN A TENT —

When camping, the outdoorsman will find a few wall pockets sewed to the tent walls at the back end provide a convenient means to hold the soap, mirror, razor and other small articles liable to be lost. The pockets can be made of the same material as the tent.

CHAPTER 2

CAMPSITE BASICS

MASTERING *the* GREAT OUTDOORS

— THE TRICKS OF CAMPING OUT —

When summer comes, thousands of city dwellers feel the call of the outdoors and the lure of camp life, which means a restful, gypsy-like existence far from crowds and noisy streets. To the man who knows the tricks or the "art" of camping, several weeks in a tent is a carefree experience. The knowledge

FINDING A LEVEL SITE.

of how to live in the woods means the difference between comfort and discomfort after leaving behind the world of gas stoves, spring beds, and refrigerators.

The outdoor fan who chooses to put a canvas roof over his head on the bank of a stream or lake is on "his own." He must know a few things

FACE TENT AWAY FROM WIND

forest primeval, but the experienced outdoorsman shuns such a site in the summertime, as he wants his camp to be bathed with sunshine part of the day and also swept by breezes. Therefore, a high, well-drained spot on a river bank or one jutting out in a lake or stream and not too densely covered with trees is an ideal location for the permanent camp.

about choosing a campsite. He should know how to fix up his camp for comfort, keep perishable foods, make a bough bed, and other things that contribute to the success of his "back-to-nature" existence.

The first problem that confronts the tent dweller when he arrives in vacationland is the choice of a campsite. Where the tent shall be pitched is an important matter. Briefly, the trick of "getting set" in a tent home involves the following: pure drinking water; a fairly level spot for the tent; an ample supply of firewood; exposure that ensures sunlight part of the day; and drainage. The inexperienced camper may dream about his ideal camp buried in the heart of the

And which way shall the tent be faced? As a rule an easterly exposure is best. Next comes the southeasterly exposure. In any event, face your tent away from that point of the compass that is apt to produce heavy blows and squalls. After the camper has scanned the landscape for the best site, found the high ground, and is ready to make his decision, the common blunder usually made is to pitch the tent under a big tree. The big tree may be all right when there's blue sky overhead, but during a storm it's another story. Avoid the big ones, especially those with dead limbs that may

LOCATING PURE DRINKING WATER.

TRENCHING

light mean damp food, damp blankets or sleeping bag, unhealthy sleeping conditions, and eventually mildewed equipment. Unobstructed sunlight on your tent for several hours every day is almost a necessity if one is to be comfortable and healthy during the period spent in the woods.

come hurtling down upon you some night.

If you are in a country that offers few fairly level spots, smooth off the floor area of your future outdoor home and cut a narrow trench around the outside of it. This should be close to the wall of the tent, about 3 in. deep and 3 or 4 in. wide. In case of a heavy rain any water having an inclination to drain down the slope into your quarters will be caught by this "trough" and diverted.

For a permanent camp, a site in dense timber into which the sunlight can hardly penetrate is to be avoided. The average city dweller who goes into the woods for his first camping experience is apt to think of shade first of all as he selects a spot for his tent. All shade and no sun-

Anchoring a tent in terrain that has little topsoil, thus making it difficult to drive the tent pegs into the ground, presents a problem that can be solved by using large logs over the guy ropes. Drive in the pegs as far as possible and then swing the ax on a log to cut a chunk to fit your needs. Roll this wood over the guy ropes next

KEEP AWAY FROM EXCESSIVE SHADE.

to the pegs, and it will back up the stakes in their work of holding your tent against wind. If a wall tent is used, one can dispense with the small pegs commonly used to hold the walls to the ground by having more logs or big boulders. Allow several inches of the

SECURING GUY ROPES

wall to rest on the ground. Place your logs or boulders over this and you won't need pegs.

The camper needs a tool kit to make himself comfortable in the woods. To make rough camp furniture, cut wood, and repair equipment the following items should be taken into the woods: a good ax; hatchet; a spade (for trenching the tent, digging a refuse pit, etc.); a hammer; an assortment of nails; a ball of heavy twine; about 20 ft. of heavy wire for hooks; 1 spool of annealed wire; a small saw (if you wish to make your camp table and other furniture); and a coil of heavy sash cord or ¼-in. rope. With these

tools one can play carpenter and in a few hours have an array of equipment that will make for orderliness, comfort and health.

For example, it is uncomfortable to eat while sitting on the ground, so the first job is to build a table if a folding dining table is not included in the camp equipment. Here is where the man handy with tools earns his salt the very first day in camp. He can drive four stakes into the ground for legs, nail cleats across the ends, and then proceed with the top. If one has a few packing cases in camp, the top of the table can be made from them. If

BUILDING A CAMP TABLE.

UTENSIL RACK

shipshape and making some of the following things for his outdoor home. First, a rack for the cooking utensils, which can be made as follows: Drive two forked sticks into the ground until they are about 30 in. high. Lay a pole, 4 or 5 feet long and 2 or 3 in. in diameter, across these. Wire or nail the ends of the pole to the supports. Then dig up that coil of heavy wire and make 5 or 6 S-hooks to be hung on the pole.

boards are not available, straight sticks will do. When finished, the table should be about 30 in. high. Benches for it can be made in the same manner. A tent fly, tarpaulin, or other fabric spread over this table completes the job.

With these in place, you have a rack for the skillets, cooking pots, coffee pot, and other cooking utensils. If there is a tree close to the "kitchen," it can be converted into a rack by nailing to the trunk inverted crotches.

The disorderly camper strews his equipment around, can never find anything, ignores his food supplies and then wonders why camping is more work than play. The orderly tent dweller spends several hours the first day getting things

TOWEL RACK

In the commissary tent (and every camping party should have a small tent for this purpose, with an awning to work and cook under in wet weather) we used a trimmed bush as a rack for the dishtowels, etc. Ten

CLOTHES RACK

then lay poles on them. Drive nails in these poles 6, 8, or 10 in. apart or make some more wire hooks for them, and you have hooks aplenty on which to hang things.

The advantage of this arrangement is apparent when bedtime comes around. One can undress, hang his clothes high and dry and in the morning simply reach up for his outfit, which has been kept out of the dirt and dampness. Guns and fishing rods can be cared for in much the same manner by forked sticks and poles placed closer to the ground. These articles may be ruined if left to lie on the floor of the tent. A rack built outside of the tent is handy thing for fishing rods during the day, but these delicate accessories should not be left out overnight.

Manufacturers have devised many ingenious types of lanterns and other lighting equipment for the camper, but there often comes a time when the old candle must serve after the sun goes down. They are a nuisance and a menace unless fitted into a candleholder that keeps them standing straight up. A tin can makes a serviceable candleholder if it

minutes will do the trick. Take your ax, go into the woods, find a bush with a number of branches and cut it down. Then trim it so that the stubs of the branches will remain. Drive this skeleton into the ground where you want it, and you have an excellent rack for the dishtowels.

A camping party that stays more than one or two nights in one place should fit up the sleeping tent with a little rustic equipment that can be made quite easily. Where to hang things is always a problem for the city man who comes fresh from a world of closets, coat hangers, and furniture with capacious drawers. Here is the way to take care of the clothes, guns, tackle, and other things in the sleeping tent so that they won't be cluttering up the quarters: If you are using a wall tent, sink a forked stick in each corner and is filled with moist earth. Tamp it down around the candle and you will have lighting equipment fit to be used.

Although it's thrilling to read about the woodsman who rises with the sun, strides down to the crystal brook and plunges his face into the water to perform his morning ablutions, the average

CANDLESTICK

camper prefers a more convenient setup, which involves a wash stand. If two trees are standing fairly close together, one can make a shelf out of sticks and a few nails on which the washbasin can be placed; if a small box is available this is still better. If the back-to-nature method of washing in the lake or stream is preferred, better give the bar of soap a

fair shake by at least making a soap container as follows: Drive a stake into the ground near the water and nail into its top a small piece of birch bark, the top of a tin box, or a flattened tin can that will serve as a soap dish.

In tackling the problems of keeping perishable food fresh in camp or sleeping comfortably, the city dweller camping for the first time is apt to be stumped. Food especially is a stickler. Here are some tricks that can be worked to keep such articles as butter, milk, or fresh meat cool with the use of ice. In the first place, use friction-top tins for butter, lard, and similar food articles. These can be purchased at any sporting-goods store. Secondly, make a sort of an "icebox" for your perishables. If you have a spring near camp, your cooling box can be placed in it. Take an ordinary packing box such as the grocer will use to pack your supplies and put it down 2, 3, or 4 in. in the spring or in the rivulet that flows from a spring. There should be two or more

WASH STAND

holes in each end of the box near the bottom of it so that the cool water can flow through. Place the tin of butter, the can of lard, or other foodstuffs on the flat rocks inside of the box, and even in the warmest weather things will keep cool.

KEEPING FOOD COOL

This back-to-nature type of icebox has only one drawback. It may be a lure for prowling mammals, so it is wise to keep the top fastened down. A big rock will do the trick. Although this spring box will keep milk, butter, and other things cool and sweet, it won't keep them from being tainted if you put fish in the cooler, because the former picks up odors from the fish. If you are not near a spring, dig a hole in the moist earth for the box.

CAMP STOVE

If you should be one of those fortunate campers in a not too remote area where ice can be had, you'll have to go to the nearest town for a barrel before you start to work on your icebox. A good-sized barrel is the simplest ice chest that can be devised for camp.

Provide a couple holes in the bottom of it for drainage, put the ice in the bottom and you're prepared for any temperature.

To hold such foodstuffs as beans, rice, flour, sugar, salt, and similar items there is nothing like the waterproof bags that can be purchased in nearly any sporting-goods store. They are tough, will stand punishment, do not absorb moisture, and can be obtained in any size. When labeled, they are ideal for carrying foodstuffs.

At least one-third of a camper's time is spent in bed, so the matter of sleeping arrangements in camp cannot be overlooked. One can stand most any kind of a hardship during the day, but when night comes there is just one thing that will keep a man going, and that is restful sleep on a good bed. The camper has a wide range of bedding materials and outfits to choose from, including folding camp cots, sleeping bags, bough beds, and air mattresses, all of which are recommended. The trick of keeping warm on a camp cot is in having more blankets

under you than over you, because there is a big circulating air space between you and the floor of the tent that "draws" the body heat.

Air mattresses make soft beds, but they need several layers of woolen-blanket insulation. While on an Alaskan big-game hunt, the campers carried air mattresses on the entire trip, but with plenty of spruce boughs available for beds, they stuck to the latter. With a sleeping bag for warmth their sleeping facilities were top-notch.

Every camper should know how to make a browse bed even though he is in a permanent camp with cots, springs, or other appurtenances of civilization. Here is the method and, if followed, it will produce a springy,

STRAW MATTRESSES

A BOUGH BED

the hard stems will be burrowing underneath.

After covering the ground with a mat of this sort you're ready for the second operation. With the hatchet, cut a plentiful supply of smaller branches, just long enough to keep their heads above the first layer when stuck through it. Pad the bed from one end to the other with these. If time permits, go over the bed with another layer of small twigs because a browse bed is soft and springy in proportion to the time and material used on it.

fragrant bed. First the material. Let the poet sing of his "bed of pine boughs," but when you select material for your browse bed look for hemlock or balsam trees as your sources of material.

Cedar and spruce will serve very well, but pine-tree branches are quite hopeless because they haven't the bulk. With an ample supply of short twigs, start at the foot or the head of your bed where short logs staked down will help to keep the boughs in place. Stick the twigs in the ground so that the tips will be exposed and lay a row across the bed. Then lay down row after row of the boughs so that only the tips will be in the air while

Throw your blankets or your sleeping bag on this mattress and you needn't worry about a restful night's sleep. Another good kink is to make up mattresses from ticking; just a simple bag that will fit a camp cot. Fold them up and pack them among the dunnage. When camped, fill the mattresses with hay, straw, or even dry long grass, and you will have comfortable, warm beds.

— TOURING IN THE AUTO: THE LAND CRUISER —

Because there are so many ways in which an automobile can be converted to touring purposes, and so many ideas of personal comfort and convenience to be taken into consideration, it is manifestly impossible to lay down any set rules and regulations for construction and arrangement. Much depends upon the size of the party that is making the trip; if there are not more than two, a touring-car chassis will perhaps answer. If there are to be three or more, a truck is recommended—unless, of course, the party wants to carry tents and camp out literally.

If a touring car is to be rebuilt into a traveling dwelling, the first thing that must be done is to strengthen the rear spring, if it is not already stiff enough. It must support the additional weight of the new body without letting it down against the axle every time the car goes over a bump in the road, and it may also

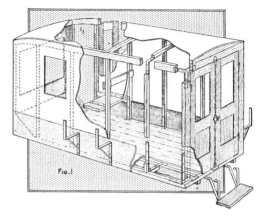

Fig. 1

THE METHOD OF FRAMING THE CAR BODY IS ILLUSTRATED HERE. THE LUGGAGE CARRIERS ARE NECESSARY FOR THE BODY SHOWN IN FIGURE 8.

be necessary to lengthen the frame by one or two feet.

Next will come the construction of a body, and here the builder gets his first opportunity to exercise his originality and ingenuity in devising new features that will add to his comfort on the road. *Figure 1* illustrates a type of body that is easily built. All corners are secured with body irons of various kinds and, if the owner is also the builder, he can have these made by "the village blacksmith" or buy them ready-made.

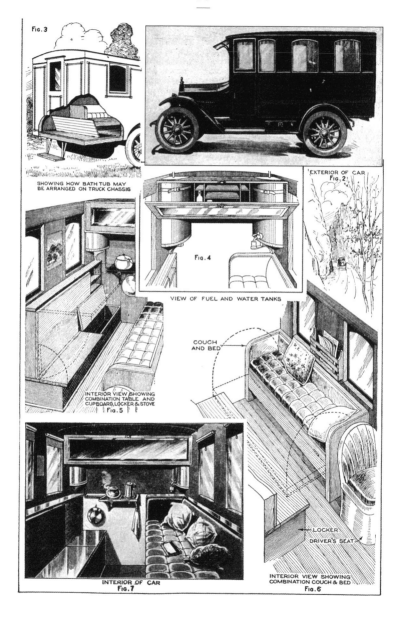

Fig. 3

SHOWING HOW BATH TUB MAY
BE ARRANGED ON TRUCK CHASSIS

EXTERIOR OF CAR
Fig. 2

Fig. 4

VIEW OF FUEL AND WATER TANKS

COUCH
AND BED

INTERIOR VIEW SHOWING
COMBINATION TABLE AND
CUPBOARD, LOCKER & STOVE
Fig. 5

LOCKER

DRIVER'S SEAT

INTERIOR OF CAR
Fig. 7

INTERIOR VIEW SHOWING
COMBINATION COUCH & BED
Fig. 6

Hardwood should be used throughout and the sides covered with plywood, or heavy wallboard suitably waterproofed. Unless the owner is an experienced "hand" and has considerable skill, it would perhaps be better and ultimately more economical to have the work done by a professional body builder. Also, ready-made bodies for both passenger and truck chassis can be bought for use on a popular make of light car.

Figure 2 shows a type of automobile that is particularly pleasing in appearance, various views of its interior arrangement being shown below.

The drawing in *Figure 3* shows an original idea of one bath-loving tourist who arranged a bathtub of his own design underneath the floor of the body. During the daytime, and when not in use, the tub served to hold the "crew's" bedding, and similar articles.

At the rear of the car are tanks for water and fuel for the stove, as shown in *Figure 4*. These tanks are placed in the corner on suitable brackets and held in place with straps, the space

between them being taken up by a locker for toilet materials, or it may be used as a storage for cooking utensils. An alternative arrangement, by means of which a larger quantity of water could be carried, would be to mount a single tank horizontally in the corner against the roof. Then again, the tank might be mounted on the outside, above or below the car.

It's worth mentioning here that the presence of a door at the rear of the car will influence the interior arrangement.

Another view of the convenient interior of this car is given in *Figure 5*. This shows the combination table and cupboard, locker, and stove. When not in use, the table serves as a door for the cupboard, and is raised to the position shown by the dotted lines when in use. The locker, which extends beyond the cupboard, serves as a support for the bed when it is opened out, as shown in *Figure 6*. Like everything else, this idea will immediately suggest variations of design and arrangement. The bed may be one of those folding ones

VARIOUS VIEWS OF THE EXTERIOR AND INTERIOR OF AN UP-TO-DATE "LAND YACHT." ALTHOUGH THE INTERIOR ARRANGEMENT IS ENTIRELY SUGGESTIVE, IT WILL BE FOUND VERY PRACTICAL AND WILL AFFORD A MAXIMUM AMOUNT OF SPACE AND COMFORT, WITHOUT ADDING TOO MUCH WEIGHT.

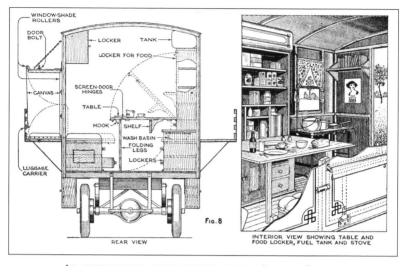

WINDOW-SHADE ROLLERS
DOOR BOLT
LOCKER
TANK
LOCKER FOR FOOD
CANVAS
SCREEN-DOOR HINGES
TABLE
HOOK
SHELF
WASH BASIN
FOLDING LEGS
LOCKERS
LUGGAGE CARRIER
REAR VIEW

FIG. 8

INTERIOR VIEW SHOWING TABLE AND FOOD LOCKER, FUEL TANK AND STOVE

AN ALTERNATIVE ARRANGEMENT OF THE "CRUISER" BODY, MORE SUITABLE FOR USE IN WARM CLIMATES. IN THIS, AS IN THE OTHER DESIGN, SPACE IS CONSERVED AS MUCH AS POSSIBLE.

best known as a "sanitary couch," fitted with wooden ends and suitably fastened to the body.

A more complete view of the interior is shown in *Figure 7*, which shows everything shipshape, as it would be on the road, with the exception that the steaming pot on the "galley" range would perhaps be endangered by careless driving. This view shows how the oil stove is connected to the fuel tank. Also, like all the other ideas, the arrangement of the stove is susceptible to considerable elaboration, and shelves on either side of the stove would also add to the convenience.

An arrangement that furnishes a maximum of interior space and sleeping accommodations is afforded by a body of the type shown in *Figure 8*. In this design, one or both sides are hinged to open up at the center, the lower half resting upon what during the day serves as a luggage carrier. Underneath the beds, which form comfortable seats when the sides are closed, provision is made for stowing clothing and other articles. With the sides in the open position, as shown in the drawing, roller curtains are pulled down at the side and across at the ends, to obtain the necessary privacy. Naturally, such an arrangement is more suitable for use in warmer parts of the country, although by altering the sleeping arrangements slightly, it could be used with equal satisfaction in any latitude and in any season.

The interior view shows the arrangement of the "mess" and "galley," the door of the cupboard or food locker forming a table when not in use as a door. Additional storage space would be obtained with no sacrifice of space by placing the stove on top of a cupboard or chest of drawers. The hinged sides of the car are held in their open and closed positions by means of chains and bolts respectively, as indicated. Of course, every spare bit of space can and should be utilized for the storage of clothing, food, and supplies. The ingenious builder, while profiting from the suggestions illustrated in these two types, will doubtless be able to devise any number of additional comforts and conveniences that will meet the special requirements of his own "crew." These designs have been stripped to the mere essentials for providing comfortable living quarters while on the road, and no attempt has been made to encumber the car with shower baths, refrigerators, or similar arrangements, the inclusion of which is left entirely to the builder.

— HOW TO MAKE A BED OF BOUGHS —

Thousands of men who camp in the woods sleep on twig beds, but it is safe to say that comparatively few know the proper way of making such a bed so that it can be slept on comfortably. The mere cutting of a mass of branches and covering it with a blanket does not make for that enviable comfort so much talked of by old campers. A single thick branch will cause a sleepless night, not to mention what an armful unevenly distributed ones will do.

There is only one way of making a twig bed that is worthwhile. The twigs selected should have stems not thicker than ¼ in., while smaller ones would be still better. Take a canvas or blanket, go to a tree, cut off a supply, and bring it in. Two men working at the job will soon have the bed ready for the night. The head of the bed should be higher than the foot, and the drawing shows how the twigs should be arranged at an angle, with the butts off the stems resting on the ground. In this manner the thick matting of the twig tops will keep the body from coming into contact with the sticks.

When completed, stretch the covering blanket over the boughs. It should be mentioned that it is a good idea to fasten straps or cords at the four corners of the covering canvas or blanket; these can be tied to the tent pegs and drawn tight.

Balsam, fir, and cedar twigs are the best materials to use for the purpose; branches from most other trees are practically useless.

— SIMPLE WAY OF TYING BOOT LACES WHEN WALKING THROUGH WEEDS —

To keep the laces of your high-top shoes or boots from becoming untied when walking through weeds and brush, tie them as shown. Loop the ends

of the laces and insert them through the upper eyelets of the shoes. Then pass opposite ends of the laces through the loops and pull them up tightly.

— ILLUMINATING THE CAMP —

Nearly every well-equipped camper carries a gasoline camp lantern, and there is usually a tripod from a camera available. These articles can be combined to give better camp illumination. Experience has taught many campers that the efficiency of the camp lantern depends largely upon getting it so placed that the light is spread evenly over the campsite. Finding such a place isn't always easy, but by putting the lantern on the tripod, an ideal installation is obtained. Merely sweat a brass nut that fits the screw in the head of the tripod to the bottom of the lantern. Light the lantern, screw it onto the tripod head and set the tripod wherever light is needed. The bottom of the camp lantern is slightly recessed to that the nut soldered to the bottom of it in no way interferes with setting the lantern down on a flat surface.

GASOLINE CAMP LANTERN ON CAMERA TRIPOD IMPROVES CAMP ILLUMINATION.

— AN OUTDOOR FIREPLACE —

A Wisconsin tinsmith has devised a neat outdoor fireplace for campers and tourists, which allows the full enjoyment of cooking over an open fireplace without annoyance from smoke. The draft caused by this device also aids in building a fire quickly. It consists of a length of 8-in. galvanized-iron pipe with a 24-in. cone at the bottom and a wind vane elbow at the top. It is supported on a length of 1¼-in. pipe, a bolt through the top of the elbow providing a pivot upon which it may turn with the wind. Two doubled lengths of strap iron are riveted at either end of the pipe on the inside to strengthen the stack and hold it in a vertical position without interfering with its operation, and these rest on washers pinned to the supporting pipe. The latter is driven into the ground inside of a short length of 3-in. pipe, and the space between the two is packed with soil or ashes. A double loop of strap iron is clamped to the top of the 3-in. pipe to hold cooking utensils.

OUTDOOR FIREPLACE ELIMINATES ANNOYANCE FROM SMOKE AND PROVIDES A GRATE OVER THE FIRE.

OUTDOOR INNOVATIONS

— SELF-EXTINGUISHING CAMP CANDLE —

To leave his candle burning so that it will safely extinguish itself at any estimated time, one camper inserts the candle in a tin can and presses the cover against it to hold it erect. As soon as the candle burns down to the cover, it drops into the can, which is partly filled with water.

LID BENT

WATER

TIN CAN

— How to Make a Canteen —

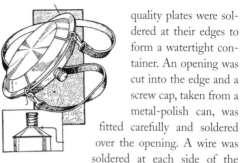

Two sheet-metal plates that are nickel-plated may be joined and provided with a suitable opening to form a useful canteen for the camper or hiker. The illustration shows such a convenience fitted with a shoulder strap ready for use.

It was made as follows: Two good-quality plates were soldered at their edges to form a watertight container. An opening was cut into the edge and a screw cap, taken from a metal-polish can, was fitted carefully and soldered over the opening. A wire was soldered at each side of the screw cap, providing loops for the snap buckles of the shoulder strap.

— Device Enables Crosscut Saw to be Used by One Man —

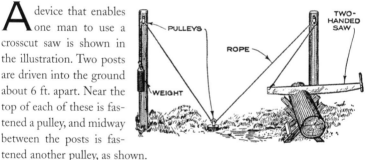

A device that enables one man to use a crosscut saw is shown in the illustration. Two posts are driven into the ground about 6 ft. apart. Near the top of each of these is fastened a pulley, and midway between the posts is fastened another pulley, as shown.

A sawhorse is placed beside one of the posts. The handle is removed from one end of the saw, and the end of a rope is passed through one of the bolt holes and tied.

The other end is passed over the pulley on the first post, under the center pulley, over the pulley on the other post, and a heavy counterweight is then fastened to it. With this arrangement, the saw may be easily handled by one man.

— CROTCHED STICK DRIVEN IN GROUND SERVES AS CAMP BOOTJACK —

Campers who wear rubber boots will find that a crotched stick will serve as bootjack to remove them. Use a strong stick and drive it into the ground at an angle as indicated in the drawing.

— STRING-CUTTING RING MADE OF HORSESHOE NAIL—

Persons having to tie a large number of packages or parcels soon find that their fingers become sore from breaking the heavy cord in the usual manner, by wrapping it around the finger to form a cutting loop. A handy device that can be easily made is a string-cutting ring fashioned from a horseshoe nail, as shown. The point of the nail is curled into a hook, and the inner edge of the hook is sharpened. The string is quickly looped around the hook and cut by a slight pull on the free end. The ring is worn on the little finger.

— GUARD FOR AX HANDLES —

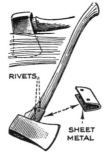

A southern lumberman, who did much timber splitting, had considerable trouble due to his ax handles wearing close to the head, causing them to break easily at this point. Consequently, he devised the simple shield shown in the drawing to prevent the trouble. The shield consisted of thin sheet iron, bent over and screwed securely to the handle as shown.

— CANDLE "FLOOR LAMP" FOR TENT MOVED ANYWHERE DESIRED —

A length of bamboo split at one end to take a candle and at the other to form three legs will provide a floor lamp for your tent. Such a lamp will enable you to have light in any part of the tent. The legs of the lamp can be pushed into the ground to help prevent it from tipping.

— ❖ ❖ ❖ —

CHAPTER 3

CATCHING
the BIG ONE

ANGLING *for a* WINNER

— TROUT FISHING WITH FLY AND BAIT —

The art of angling is generally viewed as one of the world's greatest recreations, and while each and every phase of fishing may be said to possess certain charms of its own, fly-fishing for trout is regarded by most well-informed sportsmen as the alpha and omega of the angler's art. This is so because the trout family is an uncommonly wary and game fish, and the tackle used for its capture is of finer balance and less clumsy than any employed in angling for the coarser game fishes.

If he would take full advantage of any sport and reap the greatest pleasure from a day spent in the open, it is really necessary for the sportsman to get together a good outfit. It is not essential to have a very expensive one, but it should be good of its kind, well proportioned for the purpose for which it is to be used. The beginner, who buys without good knowledge of the articles required, or fails to use careful discrimination, is almost certain to accumulate a varied assortment of junk; attractive enough in appearance, perhaps, but well nigh useless when it is tested out on the stream.

A good representative outfit, then, is of the first importance; it means making a good beginning by initiating the novice in the sport under the most favorable conditions. Let us then consider the selection of a good fishing kit, a well-balanced rod, the kind of a reel to use with it, the right sort of a line, flies, and the other few items found in the kit off the practical and experienced trout fisherman.

IF HE WOULD TAKE FULL ADVANTAGE OF ANY SPORT AND REAP THE GREATEST PLEASURE FROM A DAY SPENT IN THE OPEN, THE SPORTSMAN SHOULD GET TOGETHER A GOOD FISHING OUTFIT.

— SELECTING A GOOD FLY ROD —

The ordinary fishing pole may be bought offhand at almost any hardware store, but a well-balanced rod for fly-fishing should be well tested beforehand. The requirements call for a rod of comparatively light weight, a rod that is elastic and resilient, and yet strong enough to prove durable under the continued strain of much fishing. If the angler has made his own rod, he will have a good dependable fly rod, but the large majority of anglers who are about to purchase their first fishing kit should carefully consider the selection of the rod.

At the outset it must be understood that good tackle is simply a matter of price, the finest rods and reels are necessarily high in price,

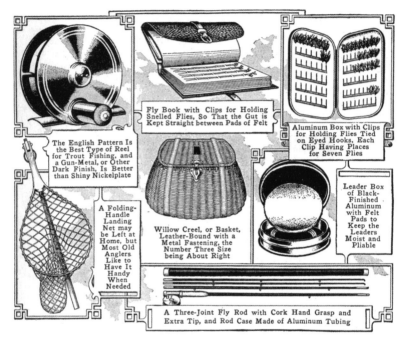

The English Pattern Is the Best Type of Reel for Trout Fishing, and a Gun-Metal, or Other Dark Finish, Is Better than Shiny Nickelplate

Fly Book with Clips for Holding Snelled Flies, So That the Gut is Kept Straight between Pads of Felt

Aluminum Box with Clips for Holding Flies Tied on Eyed Hooks, Each Clip Having Places for Seven Flies

A Folding-Handle Landing Net may be Left at Home, but Most Old Anglers Like to Have It Handy When Needed

Willow Creel, or Basket, Leather-Bound with a Metal Fastening, the Number Three Size being About Right

Leader Box of Black-Finished Aluminum with Felt Pads to Keep the Leaders Moist and Pliable

A Three-Joint Fly Rod with Cork Hand Grasp and Extra Tip, and Rod Case Made of Aluminum Tubing

and the same thing may be said of lines and flies. Providing the angler has no objection to paying a fairly high price for a rod, the choice will naturally fall upon the handmade split bamboo. For a fair amount of money a good quality fly rod may be purchased. The question may arise, is a split-bamboo rod necessary? The sportsman's long experience says that it is not, and that a finely made solid-wood rod, of greenheart or dagame, is quite as satisfactory in the hands of the average angler as the most expensive split bamboo. A good rod of this sort may be had fairly inexpensively, and with reasonable care ought to last a lifetime.

The points to look for in a fly rod, whether the material is split bamboo or solid wood, is an even taper from the butt to the tip. That is, the rod should register a uniform curve or arc over the entire length. For general fly casting 9 ft. is a handy length, and a rod of 6½ oz.

weight will prove more durable than a lighter tool. A good elastic rod is wanted for fly casting, but a too willowy or whippy action had best be avoided. However, for small-brook fishing long casts, a somewhat shorter and stiffer rod will be more useful.

For casting in large northern streams, where the current is swift and trout run to a larger size, a 9½ or 10-ft. rod of 8 oz. weight is often preferred. Of course, the veteran angler can safely use a much lighter rod than the beginner, and one occasionally meets a man on the stream that uses a 5-oz. rod for pretty heavy fishing. To be on the safe side, the novice will make no mistake in choosing a rod of fair length and conservative weight.

When selecting a rod in the tackle shop, do not settle for a mere examination of the appearance, but have the dealer affix a reel of the weight and size intended to be used with it. You'll gain a very good idea of the rod's behavior by reeling on a short length of line and reeving it through the guides and then fastening the end to a weight lying upon the floor. By reeling in the line and putting tension on the rod its elasticity and curve may be seen and felt as well as in actual fishing. To give the utmost satisfaction, the rod should fit its owner; several rods should be tried until one is found that most fully meets the angler's idea of what a rod should be.

If one happens to have a good fly reel, by all means take it along and attach it to the rod while making the tests. It is practically impossible to gauge the balance of a rod without affixing the reel, and many a finely balanced tool will appear badly balanced until the proper-weight reel is affixed to it.

— THE PROPER KIND OF REEL —

For fly-fishing nothing is so good as the English style of click reel, which is made with a one-piece revolving side plate and with the handle affixed directly to it. Any kind of balanced-handle reel is an out-and-out nuisance on the fly rod, because it has no advantage in quickly recovering the line, and the projecting handle is forever catching the line while casting. In fly casting, the length of cast is regulated by the amount of line taken from the reel before the cast is made. It is while "pumping" this slack line through the guides, in making the actual cast, that the balanced or projecting handle is very apt to foul the line. A good reel that is smooth-running like a watch will cost a modest amount, but a very good one may be had for half that. Cheaper ones, while not so durable, may be used with fair satisfaction.

The heavier multiplying reels, so essential for bait casting from a free reel, are altogether unsuited for the fly rod, being too heavy when placed below the hand—the only proper position for the reel when fly casting. The single-action click reel, having a comparatively large diameter but being quite narrow between the plates, is the one to use. Hard rubber or vulcanite is a good material for the side plates, while the trimmings

may be of German silver or aluminum. The all-metal reel is of about equal merit, but whatever the material, the most useful size is one holding about 40 yards of No. E-size waterproof line. A reel of this capacity will measure about 3 in. in diameter and have a width of about ⅞ in. between plates. A narrow-spooled reel of this type enables the fisherman to reel in the line plenty fast enough.

Owing to the fact that the reel is placed below the grip on fly rods, a rather lightweight instrument is needed to balance the rod. Of the two extremes, it is better to err on the side of lightness, because a heavy reel makes a butt-heavy rod and, throwing extra weight on the wrist and arm, makes casting increasingly difficult after an hour's fishing. An old hand at the game will appreciate this point better than the novice.

— THE KIND OF LINE TO USE —

The fly-casting line used by a veteran is generally of silk, enameled, and having double taper; that is, the line is thickest in the center and gradually tapers to a smaller diameter at each end. Single-tapered lines are likewise extensively used

and, though they cost less, they are tapered at one end only and cannot be reversed to equalize the wear caused by casting. The level line, which has the same diameter throughout its entire length, is the line most generally used, but the cast cannot be so delicately made with it. For the beginner, however, the level line in size No. E is a good choice. For small-brook fishing, No. F is plenty large enough. In choosing the size of line, there is a common-sense rule among fly casters to select a line proportioned to the weight of the rod. For a light rod a light line is the rule, and for the heavier rod a stouter line is the logical choice. If the rod is of a too stiff action, use a comparatively heavy line, and it will limber up considerably; if the rod is extremely "whippy," use the lightest line that can be purchased, and it will be used with safety.

— A FINE LEADER MARKS THE EXPERT CASTER —

The leader for trout is preferably of single gut and as fine as the angler's skill will allow. The fly caster's rule is to use a leader whose breaking strain is less than the line, then, when the tackle parts, it is simply a question of putting on a new leader and the more expensive line is saved. Ready-made leaders may be purchased or the angler can tie them as desired. For length, a 3 or 3½-ft. leader is about right for average fishing. Longer leaders are used, and while they sometimes are of advantage, the 3-ft. length is more useful. A longer leader is awkward to handle because the loop is apt to catch in the top of the rod when reeling in the line to bring the fish close to the net. Leaders may be had with a loop at each end, or with loops tied in, for using a cast of two or three flies. For all average casting, the two-fly cast is the best. But the expert angler uses the single–fly very often. For lake fishing, the single large fly is generally preferred. For using two flies, the leader is provided with three loops, one at the top, another at the bottom, and an extra loop tied in about 15 in. from the lower loop. In fly casting, the first, or upper, fly is known as the "dropper," and the lower one as the "tail" fly. For the single-fly cast only two loops are required.

Gut used for leaders should be carefully selected. Only those lengths that are of uniform diameter and well rounded should be chosen; lengths that show flat and rough spots should be discarded. Dry gut that is very

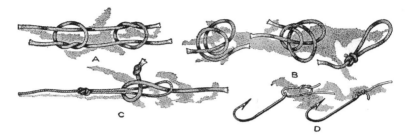

THE SINGLE WATER KNOT USED IN TYING LEADERS; A GOOD KNOT FORM MAKING THE LOOP AT THE END OF THE LEADERS; AN ANGLER'S KNOT USED FOR ATTACHING THE LINE TO THE LEADER, AND THE JAM KNOT FOR ATTACHING EYED FLIES, OR HOOKS, TO THE LEADER OR SNELL.

brittle should be handled very little, and previous to a day's fishing the leaders must be soaked in water overnight to make them pliable, then coiled in between felt pads in the leader box to keep them in fishing shape. After use, put the frayed leaders aside and dry them out between the flannel leaves of the fly book.

Gut is the product of the silkworm, and the best quality is imported from Spain. It comes in bundles, or hanks, of 1,000 strands, 10 to 20 in. long and in different thicknesses, or strengths. The heaviest are known as Royal and Imperials, for salmon; Marana, for extra-heavy bass; Padron, for bass; regular, for heavy trout; Fina, for light trout, and Refina, for extra light trout. The grades Fina and Refina are well suited for all aver-

age fly fishing, while the heavier sizes are useful for heavy large fishing.

To make the leaders, soak the strands of gut in warm water overnight until they are soft and pliable. Select the strands for each leader of the desired thickness and length so that the finished leader will have a slight taper to one end only. A nicely tapered leader of light weight can be made by using the Fina gut for the upper length and tying in two lengths of Refina gut. Begin the leader by uniting the strands together to make it the correct length, three 12-in. strands being about right for average casting. The single water knot is the strongest and neatest to use. Make it by taking the thick end of the strand and doubling it back enough to tie in a common knot just large enough for the line to pass through and drawing it up tightly. Tie a single loose knot in the other end of the strand, about ⅛ in. in diameter and close to the end; take the next thickest strand of gut, thread the thicker end through the loose knot, and tie a second square knot around the strand, as shown at *A*.

By pulling on the two long ends the loops can be drawn up tightly, and the two knots will slide together and make a neat and very strong knot.

Repeat this operation until as many strands of gut are knotted together as required to make the leader of the desired length. For making the loop at the ends, a double-bighted knot, tied as shown at *B*, is used. If a dropper fly is desired, do not pull the water knot tightly. Instead, insert a short length of gut with a common knot at the end and a loop in the other, then draw the water knot up tightly and a short snell will be made for attaching the fly as normal.

— FLIES FOR TROUT FISHING —

The standard selection of artificial flies numbers about 60, but the average fisherman will find about 24 patterns to answer every need. For making up the most "killing" flies for the trout season, the following are recommended: Use red ibis, stone fly, cinnamon, red spinner, and parchmenee belle, for April; turkey brown, yellow dun, iron blue, spinner, mont real, and red box, for May; spider, black gnat, silver doctor, gray drake, orange dun, and green drake, for June; July dun, grizzly king, pale evening dun, red ant, and brown palmer, for July; Seth green, coachman, shad, governor, August dun, and royal coachman, for August, and black palmer, willow, whirling dun, queen of the water, and blue bottle, for September.

The well-known "angler's knot" is used to attach a line to the leader. This knot is shown at *C*. The snelled fly is attached by passing the loop over the loop of the leader and inserting the fly through the leader loop. When eyed flies are used they are often attached directly to the leader, or a looped snell may be used as in the ordinary American-tied fly. To attach the eyed fly direct to the leader, the common "jam knot," shown at *D*, is mostly used. When the slipknot is drawn tightly and the extra end cut off it makes a small, neat knot, not apt to slip.

AS A GENERAL RULE, THE VETERAN FLY FISHERMAN PREFERS TO WADE
WITH THE CURRENT, AND FISHES THE WATER IN FRONT OF HIM
BY MAKING DIAGONAL CASTS ACROSS THE STREAM.

— HOW TO CAST THE FLY —

To be able to cast the artificial fly a distance of 50 ft. or more, and let the feathered lure alight upon the desired bit of water as lightly as a falling leaf, is no small accomplishment. Fly casting is an art, and to become an expert requires much practice.

The personal assistance of a skillful caster is not often available, but if the angler will follow the suggestions outlined here, a beginner will soon grasp the knack of handling the fly rod and the casting will steadily improve with practice. Just as the knack of handling a gun is best gained—not in the field, shooting live game, but through shooting at targets—so may the art of fly casting be more quickly acquired by intelligent practice conducted away from the stream, in the backyard, or any other place roomy enough to swing the rod and a moderately long line. By practicing in this way, the angler's attention is focused upon the cast and is not partly occupied with the excitement of fishing. To make a good beginning, let the reel contain about 25 yd. of common, braided, linen line (size E is about right), and instead of a fly, or hook, affix a small split shot to the end of the line. It is wise to begin with a cheap rod and save a good outfit; if the angler learns how to make a fairly long and accurate cast with a common rod, he may feel assured that he can even do better with a first-rate outfit.

The first point to observe in mak-

—FIGURE 1—
THE PROPER WAY TO TAKE HOLD
OF THE HANDLE WITH THE
REEL ON THE UNDERSIDE.

Bring the rod up slightly above the horizontal, as shown in *Figure 2*, and with a quick snap of the wrist (avoiding shoulder or body movement), throw the tip upward, checking it sharply as soon as the tip is carried over the shoulder about 25 degrees beyond the vertical plane, as in *Figure 3*. This snappy upstroke of the rod makes the "back cast" by projecting the line high in the air, and carries it well behind the angler. Before the line has fully straightened out behind, and before it has an opportu-

ing the cast is to grip the rod correctly. This is done by grasping the rod at the point where it balances best. By shifting your hand about, this point of balance is quickly found, for at no other point will the rod "hang" well in the hand. In casting, the reel is turned to the underside of the rod with the thumb extended along the top off the grip, as shown in *Figure 1*. Taking up an easy casting position, with left foot slightly advanced, pull from the reel about 25 yds. of line and let this slack line fall in coils upon the ground in front.

—FIGURE 2—
BEGIN THE CAST WITH THE ROD
IN A POSITION JUST ABOVE
THE HORIZONTAL PLANE.

—FIGURE 3—
THE ROD IS QUICKLY CHECKED
WHEN IT IS CARRIED OVER THE
SHOULDER ABOUT 25 DEGREES.

—FIGURE 4—
THE CAST IS FINISHED BY
THROWING THE LINE FORWARD
WITH A QUICK WRIST-AND-
FOREARM MOVEMENT.

nity to fall much below the caster's shoulders, the rod is snapped forward with a quick wrist-and-forearm movement. This throws the line forward in front of the fisherman and in the direction he is facing, which finishes the cast with the rod in the position shown in *Figure 4.*

Long and accurate fly casting is much more a matter of skill than muscle. And though some fly fishermen cast directly from the shoulder and upper arm, and thus use a considerable amount of muscular force in making the cast, this cannot be regarded as the best method of casting. Take full advantage of the great elasticity of the fly rod and casting will be naturally accomplished by the wrist and forearm. To make strenuous efforts to hurl the fly through the air using an arm or body movement is extremely tiring after an hour or so of fishing. If the cast is made from the wrist, aided by the forearm, the snap of the rod may be depended upon to project the fly to greater length of line and allow it to fall close to the desired spot, lightly and without splashing.

Timing the back cast is the most difficult detail of fly casting, because the line is behind the angler and the eye cannot aid the hand. The novice will soon acquire the knack of casting, however, if he will remember to keep the elbow close to the side, and to keep the line well up in the air when making the back cast. He should begin the forward movement before the line has fully straightened out behind him. After a little practice, the hand will feel the slight tension communicated to the rod as the line begins to straighten out. This should be used to correctly time the forward movement. Counting "one" for the upstroke, and "two and" for the interval required for the line to straighten out in the rear, and "three" for the forward movement, is also a good way to time the cast.

At the beginning, make no attempt to secure distance. Accuracy and delicacy in placing the fly on the water is of much more importance than length of cast in trout fishing. To this end, it is a good plan to place a newspaper about 25 ft. distant and try to drop the end of the line on this mark. When you can drop the line on the target lightly and with reasonable accuracy, you may feel justified in lengthening your cast. Casts other than the overhead cast just described are occasionally used, including the Spey, switch, wind, and flip casts. But the overhead cast is the most commonly used, although it is much more difficult to master.

To make the Spey cast, the angler requires a rapid stream that will carry the line downstream until it is straight and taut, the tip of the rod being held as long as possible to accomplish this end. The rod is then raised high in the air with a quick wrist movement, which lifts the line from the water to the extreme end. Then, without pausing, the rod is carried upstream with just sufficient force to let the fly fall just above the angler. The line is now on the reverse, or upper, side of the fisherman. With a sweep of the rod the line is projected over the water's surface—not along the surface—in the manner used in making the overhead cast.

The switch cast is sometimes useful when trees or rocks are immediately behind the fisherman, thus preventing the line from extending far enough backward to make the overhead cast. In making this cast, the line is not lifted from the water but merely to the surface by raising the tip of the rod. The line is dragged through the water by carrying the tip in the direction one is standing until it is far in the rear as the obstruction will permit. The line is projected by a quick downward sweep of the rod with sufficient force to roll it forward in a large coil or loop, much as a wheel rolls on a track.

The wind cast is a modification of the switch cast, but easier to make. Bring the line almost to your feet, and with a quick downward motion of the rod, throw the line in a long loop against the wind.

The underhand and the flip casts are so simple that it seems almost unnecessary to describe them. Both are short casts and are only used when the angler is fishing in an overgrown stream. The underhand cast is really a side cast in as much as the short line is lifted from the water in a loop and propelled in the desired direction by a side sweep of the rod. The flip cast is made by holding the fly between the thumb and finger and with a few coils of line in the right hand. Bend the rod like a bow, release the fly suddenly, and the snap of the rod will project it in the desired direction and allow it to drop lightly like a fly.

— HANDLING THE FLIES IN THE WATER —

As a general rule the veteran fly fisherman prefers to wade with the current and fishes the water in front of him by making diagonal casts across the stream. A good fisherman will systemically cover every inch of good water and little will be left to chance. The novice is inclined to fish his flies in a contrary manner, he casts more or less at random, and is as likely to splash the flies recklessly about in the most impossible places as he is to drop them in a favorable riffle or pool.

To be able to pick out fishable water, the angler should know something about the habits of trout, their characteristics at the several seasons of the fishing year, and their habits, which differ greatly in different streams. A fishing knowledge of the stream to be visited is valuable, but if the angler knows how to make a fair cast and possesses average skill in handling flies on water, there should be no question but that he will creel a fair number of trout even though he casts in strange waters.

To imitate the action of the natural insect is the most successful manner of fishing the flies, and as the natural fly will struggle more or less when borne down with the current, the fisherman endeavors to duplicate this movement by making his artificial fly wriggle about. This motion must not be overdone, for if the flies are twitched and skipped about, or pulled against the current, the wary trout will refuse to fall for any such obvious deceit. A gentle motion of the wrist will cause the fly to move somewhat as the natural insect will struggle.

Do not cast directly down or upstream but across the current at an angle. Let the flies fall upon the water as lightly as possible so that the water will carry them downstream over the likely places where the trout are hiding. Keep the line as taut as possible by drawing the slack in with the left hand. The flies should not be allowed to soak in the water, neither should they be retrieved in haste. The experienced fly caster will invariably fish with a wet line, that is to say, with a slightly submerged fly, and will let the flies drag over as much water as possible before making a second cast.

Owing to the fact that trout lie with their noses pointing upstream awaiting their food carried down by the current, the caster will naturally take pains to float his flies downstream with the leader fairly taut. To neglect this detail and allow the leader to float in a wide loop near or before the flies is slovenly fishing, and few trout will strike a fly presented in this amateurish fashion.

Early in the fishing season, and when the stream is flooded and discolored after a heavy rain, it is wise to fish the flies below the surface. Fishing in this manner makes it more difficult to tell when to strike a fish, and some little practice is needed to determine the opportune moment by feeling the slight tension on the line. Many fish will be pricked to be sure, but some trout will be creeled, and fishing with the submerged fly is sometimes the only way trout can be taken.

On fair days and in smooth water, better luck may be expected when the fly is kept upon the surface, and this is easily managed by keeping the tip of the rod well in the air. Often the fisherman can take advantage of a bit of floating foam, and if the fly is cast upon it and allowed to float with it downstream, the ruse will often prove effective.

The trout is a hard striker, and it is not unusual to have a trout rush ahead of the fly in his attempt to mouth it. In rapid water the savage rush of the fish is sufficient to hook it securely. But when casting in quiet pools, the hook is imbedded by a snap of the wrist. At what exact moment to strike, as well as the amount of force to use, depends upon circumstances. When fishing in small streams and brooks where the trout run small, much less force is necessary to hook the fish. In quiet water and in larger streams where 2 or 3-lb. trout are not uncommon, the fish may be struck with a smart upward jerk of the forearm and wrist. The matter of striking is governed by the temperament as well as the judgment of the angler. The deliberate thinking man is likely to strike too late, while the nervous individual, striking too early, is apt to prick the trout and roll him over.

The best time to fish for trout is when they are feeding on the surface. Early in spring, when there are few flies about during the warmer part of the day, say, from 10 in the morning to 5 in the afternoon, will prove to be the most successful time. Later on, when flies are numerous, you can expect good luck early in the morning. In the hot summer months the cooler hours of the day are best. Of course, there are many exceptions, because there are many cool days in summer, as well as exceptionally warm days in spring, and these changes of weather should be considered. However, extremes are not likely to make good fishing, and the trout will not rise as freely on cold, windy days, nor will they fight as gamely. On hot days, too, not so much luck can be expected during the hours of the greatest heat—12 to 4—but a good basket of trout may be creeled early in the morning or late in the afternoon of summer. A bright, clear day is usually the best for fly-fishing, because the sun brings out more flies. But a warm rain, or even a fog, is also considered good fishing weather.

— KINDS OF BAIT —

Among the live baits available for trout fishing are the minnow, white grub, cricket, grasshopper, and other insects, and last, but by no means least, the common angle or earthworm.

The minnow is beyond a doubt the most enticing morsel that can be offered to a hungry trout, and a minnow may be reckoned to secure a rise when other baits fail. The inconvenience of transporting this bait is a great drawback, and because minnows are delicate fish, a minnow bucket is necessary for their preservation. This means a lot of trouble, because the water must be frequently changed or aerated. This labor, together with the difficulty of carrying a bulky pail through the brush, makes this desirable bait almost impossible for stream and brook fishing. The saltwater minnow, known as a "shiner" or "mummychug," is top-notch trout bait. It is much tougher than the fresh water minnow, making it bait often used by anglers residing near the seacoast.

The white grub, or larvae of the so-called May beetle, is good bait available for early-season fishing and may be obtained in the early spring months by spading up grassland. The grub is about 1 in. long, and has a creamy yellow color with a darker head. It may be kept a month or more, by putting it in a box with a number of pieces of fresh turf.

Crickets, grasshoppers, and many other insects make good bait, and the earthworm is a good all-around bait for trout. A supply dug some days before and kept by packing in fresh moss and slightly moistening with milk and water will prove more attractive and the worms will be tougher and cleaner to handle than when carried in earth.

Other good baits include the fin of a trout. If this is used in combination with the eye of the same fish, it forms an attractive lure. In using this bait, do not puncture the eyeball, but hook through the thin flexible skin surrounding the eye. A fat piece of salt pork, cut into pieces 1 in. long and ¼ in. wide, makes a fairly good bait. Spoons and other spinning baits are presumably attractive, but few sportsmen use them when angling for so fine a fish as trout.

— ICE-FISHING SEMAPHORE SHIFTS BALANCE WHEN LINE IS PULLED —

Many ice-fishing signals move or wag only when the fish jerks at the line, and then return to their normal position. This one, however, continues to show that there has been a bite, even after the line has again become slack. A 1-in. cross arm having a numbered tin-can lid at one end is pivoted in a balanced position on a vertical support, which is driven into the ice. A slot is cut in the center of the cross arm to take a steel ball, which should be free to roll in the slot after two pieces of sheet metal are tacked on either side to retain it. A spool to wind up the line is fitted into a cutout in the vertical piece, and the line is threaded through screw eyes as shown. When the fine end of the cross arm is pushed down, the ball rolls toward this end and its weight keeps the cross arm in this position. When a

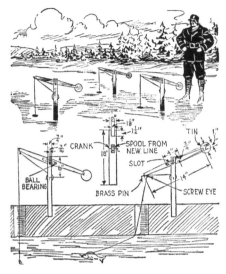

fish tugs at the line, the other end of the arm goes down so that the ball rolls toward the latter end and keeps the cross arm in this position.

— ALARM FOR ICE FISHING AT NIGHT —

Fishing through holes in the ice at night, when ordinary signal flags or tipups are invisible, is possible with the electrically illuminated device illustrated. As shown, a round stick of the desired length has a miniature lamp and

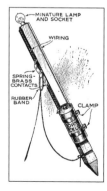

socket attached to the outer end. This is connected to a dry cell, which is clamped near the lower, pointed end. Spring-brass contacts are secured to the stick with screws, as shown. In use, the device is propped over a hole in the ice and the line is set to pass through a rubber band that separates the contacts. As soon as a fish takes the hook the band is pulled out from between the contacts, and the lamp is lighted.

— SEINE WILL CATCH CRAYFISH IN WEEDY PONDS AND STREAMS —

The difficulty of seining crayfish from a pond or stream that contains vegetation, where they are usually plentiful, is eliminated with this seine. It consists of a wooden scoop having a burlap sack at the rear end. If the seine has a tendency to float or not rest heavily enough on the bottom of the pond to flatten the growth as it is pulled along, weight it with a stone or heavy piece of metal. Drilling a number of small holes in the bottom of the scoop will also help it to sink to the bottom.

GUNNY SACK HOOKED OVER HEADLESS NAILS
1 FT.
4 FT.

— HOW TO WIND A ROD —

Here is a chance to own a real fishing rod. All you need is a long piece of bamboo, cut to the length you like. If bamboo is not available, any type of wood that has a certain flexibility will serve the purpose. The principles of winding to make a high-class rod are described simply. Follow each step carefully and take notice of the illustrations.

Although it is somewhat exacting work, anyone with a little patience

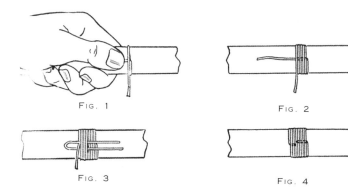

FIG. 1

FIG. 2

FIG. 3

FIG. 4

can learn to wind a rod. Put a spool on a nail and drive the nail into a block of wood. Bend the nail slightly to secure a desired tension and place the spool or spools at your right. Mark the places for guides and in-between winding on the flat or top side of rod.

Hold the rod in the left hand with one end supported between the elbow and body. The right hand is to assist the left in holding and turning it and to guide the silk on the rod.

About three inches from the end of the silk, loop it around the rod to the left with the loose end extending toward you *(Figure 1)*. The portion of the silk extending to the spool should overlap the loose end. Place the tip of a finger where they cross and turn the stick until you see it is

going to hold. During the winding the silk must be kept tight *(Figure 2)*.

After about three complete turns of the rod, take a razor blade or a sharp knife and trim the loose end close to the last turn of the silk. Take this small piece and fold it back against itself making a loop. Place this between the rod and the thread extending to the spool with the loop end toward you *(Figure 3)*. Continue to wind over this loop for at least three turns, then place thumb on the silk to keep it from unwinding, and cut the thread about two inches from the rod. Insert the loose end through the loop and pull it back under the winding. Pull the end carefully to be sure the winding is tight, then cut off as close to the silk as possible, in order not to injure the winding *(Figure 4)*.

— FISHING WITH AN UMBRELLA —

Make a handy net for catching killifish, one that can be neatly folded and readily carried in a fishing–rod bag, by re-covering an old discarded umbrella frame with mosquito netting.

Although primarily intended for catching "killies" by placing a few cracked clams or mussels in its center and lowering in shallow water not over 2 ft. deep, it can also be used for catching the beautiful silver-banded spearing by baiting it with a few pieces of shrimp. Tie the pieces to the frame near the center and suspend the net in deeper water near a sod bank. When codfish and flounders are running, the net, baited with shrimp, can be used from the end of a dock. One must be patient, allowing the net to remain down for some time before drawing it up, but when the fish are present at all, the number taken at one haul will more than make up for the time spent in waiting.

An old umbrella is also very convenient in "bobbing" for eels at night. String a dozen or more worms on strong thread, winding them up into a ball and wrapping the thread well around the mass. Let the ball sink to the bottom and when you feel a bite, draw in the line and shake the eel off into the umbrella, which has previously been hung over the side of the dock.

— HINTS FOR THE FISHERMAN —

Just as the hunter who sallies forth to the game fields must have his gun and outfit in order if he wishes to get the best results, and just as the automobilist must prepare for a tour and carry spare tires and a few tools for repairs, so the fisherman with designs upon the big ones of his favorite lake or stream should have his tackle in the best condition if he wants the most fun out of his sport. A loose ferrule that may bring trouble when a fish is played, a poorly wrapped rod tip or a reel that is dirty and not working properly, may spell the ruin of a day's sport with bass, pike, muskellunge, or trout. The wise fisherman puts the taboo on these annoyances by a few hours of work before the "battle" with the big fish begins.

If you are planning on fixing up

"Old Faithful," your pet fishing rod that has served you on many a trip, here are a few tips on how to make your wooden weapon look like new irrespective of whether it cost three, five, or seventy-five dollars. First, remove the guides by cutting through the windings. An old razor blade or a keen knife will do this trick. Take off the tip and the ferrules. If they do not come off easily, apply a little heat to the metal (by means of a match, if nothing else is handy) to easily solve the problem.

In fixing up a rod for a fishing season it is wise to remove all the silk windings and all the varnish. By scraping the stick with a sharp steel edge (such as part of the blade of an old hunting knife taped in two places so that it may be gripped) the old varnish can be removed easily but one should be careful not to scrape too hard because you must preserve the enamel on the bamboo, especially where the various parts of the rod are joined. If your rod is solid wood such as hickory or bethabara, this "manicuring" operation does not need to be done so carefully, because there is no danger of injury to any enamel.

The next operation is sandpapering. Buy the finest sandpaper that you can obtain and find a small flat block of wood, 4 or 5 in. long and about 2 in. wide. Spread a piece of sandpaper over this block and then use plenty of elbow grease as you rub down the rod. But don't bear down too hard if you're working on a bamboo rod, because the slogan is,

"remember the thin enamel coat on the bamboo must be preserved." After giving the rod a thorough rubbing down, wipe it clean so that it will be shipshape for the next operation.

This next step is where many fishermen make a fatal error, as far as the appearance of their rods is concerned. They put on a coat of varnish instead of shellac, which results in a messy job because the color preservative that will be used later on the silk wrappings turns varnish white, and presto!—the job is ruined. So the trick is to apply a light coat of good shellac first so that you have a solid foundation to work on.

In cementing the tip and ferrules to the rod, fishermen can use a wide variety of materials. Marine glue, sealing wax or ferrule cement are a few of the ingredients available. Probably best is the regular ferrule cement that can be purchased in any

sporting goods store. It comes to you a hard, brittle (when cold) stick of waxlike substance wrapped something like a big stick of candy. When you're ready to use it on the rod scrape the wood free of any of the old cement, then heat both the wood and metal, melt a little of the cement, smear it on and then shove the parts on firmly. As soon as they have cooled sufficiently you're ready to proceed with your job.

Winding the rod and fitting the guides are the next items to be tackled. Guides should be placed in position and held there either by thread or small rubber bands. Wind your gay-colored silk thread tightly and evenly toward the agate, which will assure a neat, even job. Practically every home rod worker uses the following method in winding a guide. In starting the thread he turns in one end of it so that three or four turns are passed over it (*Figure 1*). When nearly finished with the winding, the

FIG. 1

LOOP

FIG. 2

FASTENING
THE WINDINGS

FIG. 3

next trick is to throw a loop of thread on the side of the rod (*Figure 2*) so that three or four turns can be made over this loop. Then put the end of the thread through this loop (*Figure 3*), pull the end through and cut it.

Every fisherman who owns a fishing rod of wood that is gaily yet tastefully decorated with colored silk wants the windings to look good. To achieve this end note the following suggestions, designed to keep the colors of the silk bright and clear

after the varnish is applied. Any drug store can furnish the combination; banana oil and collodion in equal parts. Use a good camel's-hair brush and put on several coats of this color preservative (at least three, and four are better) and then you can varnish your rod without fear of discoloring the silk windings.

The next step is varnishing. A good grade of spar varnish, a fairly warm room for the work, a good brush that doesn't shed hairs, and

plenty of patience are the big factors in the success of this operation. Put on three or four thin coats, always allowing the rod to dry for several days between each application. If you can keep the rod in a room free of dust, it will come out looking like a million dollars and quite ready for some tussles with big fish.

Thousands of fishermen prefer steel rods for their "weapons" while on fishing trips, as these sturdy tools require little or no "petting," and can be abused more than a bamboo, hickory, or bethabara rod. As a rule there are no colored silk windings to worry about and hence home work on these steel "whips" is a negligible item. If agate guides are used on your rod, the main thing is to examine them closely after the winter storing period to see if they are intact. A cracked agate means a cut line and poor casting.

The reel is an important item in the fisherman's kit, so don't slight it when polishing things up for a trip. Take it apart carefully for cleaning. Put a drop or two of the finest lubricating oil on the vital parts and it is ready for use. Tissue paper is much better for cleaning the delicate parts of a reel than rags, because the lint from the latter can be injurious to the finely attuned parts of any baitcasting reel, whether cheap or expensive.

After the outfit is cleaned, revamped, polished and all ready for strenuous combat with the finny tribes, its worthwhile to keep in mind a few don'ts if the outfit is to stand the gaff, and last for one or more vacations. We might call these "don'ts" the ten commandments for successful Waltonians. They apply to the fisherman with a modest outfit as well as to the angler with hundreds of dollars invested in expensive tackle.

If you're fishing along a river, or on the bank of a lake don't lay your rod on the ground unless you're sure you are only fisherman in the territory. Stand the rod against a tree or in some brush so that no one can come along and step on it. Sand (or foreign particles of any kind) in a reel will ruin it. So don't carry your reel loose in your pocket, in the bait box, or in a suitcase where it may pick up some dirt. It's wise to use a

small leather case for a pet reel. A small pouch with drawstrings is also good and can be made at home at practically no cost. After fishing in the rain, dry your rod, reel and line.

The reel should be wiped with a dry cloth and a few drops of oil applied. See that all moisture is removed from the rod. Unwind all the line on your reel and let it dry out thoroughly before you start out again. Don't use a knife blade in trying to unsnarl a "backlash" on your casting reel. Backlashes (better known as "bird's nests"!) should be treated with a button hook or better yet a hairpin, neither of which has cutting edges. Don't let anybody step on your line when you're in a boat, on the shore or anywhere else. The plunk of a big outdoor boot on a fishing line is almost as bad as using a knife on it.

A step doesn't break the line at the time, but it is apt to part a little later when you have a whopping big fish on it. Don't leave your rods or reels out overnight. The soaking they will take from the dew is almost as injurious as that received in a rain. Another point is this: if the joints of your fishing rod fit rather tight, don't twist the joints when you take them apart. Separate them by a straight pull and begin with the tip. Tight-fitting ferrules can be "eased up" by rubbing with a piece of emery paper. Don't take your rod apart and toss the pieces on the ground, because sand in the ferrules means trouble. When walking through the brush with your rod don't carry it tip first. Grasp it just above the butt so that the point trails behind you waist high. Many a steel rod has been ruined and many a wooden rod broken by ramming the tip into trees. Never stand a rod or any of your tackle (reel, hip boots, lures, lines, etc.) near a hot stove or a radiator. Keep these things away from heat if you want them to last.

No matter how careful one is when on a fishing trip there may be an accident. Hence, the wise fisherman carries a little emergency repair outfit so that he can make a quick repair in the field. One day last summer, just two hours before taking a train for home, a fisherman was on a small lake trying to get a mess of black bass to take back with him. A light rain had started to fall and the bass were hitting. With his time limited, he was casting for all he was worth because fish were wanted badly and in a hurry. And then trouble stepped into the picture. He was using an inexpensive wooden rod. It cracked just above the ferrule, a decided fracture that would not permit him to even land a minnow unless repairs were made right away.

But his emergency kit came to his rescue. Out came the tape, ordinary rubber tire tape. He wrapped the tip with this and in five minutes he was ready to take on any bass. With this repaired rod he hooked and landed eight good-sized black bass and called it a day,

The fisherman can't foresee accidents but he can be ready for them with a pocket repair kit. On a long canoe and fishing trip that will take one far away from a base of supplies or tackle shop, it is wise to tuck in the duffel bag some or all of the following items: Lest the rubber boots fail take a small amount of rubber cement and rubber cloth; to repair a snag in your boot apply just a small amount of cement, put on the patch and then lay a stone, your tackle box or other heavy weight over it. This trick ensures a repair job that will hold for a long time.

Practically every fisherman using wooden fishing rods carries along tire tape and ferrule cement. Both cost little, take up practically no space, and are invaluable in repair jobs. A fisherman is still using an old bamboo rod that cost but six dollars four years ago, although twice on trips to secluded lakes, reached by long hikes, he has broken the tip of this rod and had to make emergency repairs. Each time the break did not spoil his fishing, because the lateral splice that can be made with tire tape saved the day. The stunt is simple. When the tip breaks, place the broken ends side by side for 1½ or 2 in., and then bind them with tire tape. Such a repair will hold although it is temporary and you will have to eventually replace the tip. With the tire tape take along the ferrule cement. If your rod should develop a loose ferrule, heat it with a match, remove it from the wood, clean both the wood and the metal, and then apply the melted cement. Take time out while it cools and you're then ready for more fishing.

A little pocket repair kit should have the following articles that are "standing by" for trouble: A small flat file, a pair of wire-cutting forceps, a pair of baby pliers, a roll of tire tape for hastily repairing a long break, some rubber cement and cloth for repairing rubber boots or rubber packs, a couple of feet of light copper wire so that in case one of the guides on a steel or bamboo rod is broken

you can make a new one out of wire, and ferrule cement.

Consider the addition of a piece of ordinary laundry soap to this kit, because in a pinch it will do for repairing leaks. After traveling fifteen miles to a muskellunge lake with an Indian guide, a fisherman secured a canoe and started out upon the lake for a wonderful day's sport. But the canoe leaked like a sieve. In the rickety old tumbledown boathouse where the canoe had been stored he found, after quite a search, a chunk of laundry soap. With it he filled the cracks in this manner: first moistening the places, he rubbed the cake of soap over them until a thin layer was deposited. The water could not flow through this, and after ten or fifteen minutes of work with the laundry bar he went after the muskies. Moreover he kept his feet dry while doing it, because the holes in the canoe were plugged quite thoroughly by his repair work.

There are tricks in every trade and fishing is no exception. Checking up on your outfit before you start on a trip, packing along a simple little repair kit so to be ready for accidents, and observance of a few commonsense rules in the care of tackle, not only mean saving money but success when a big one grabs the lure and starts a fight. Faulty, neglected tackle can't cope with the big fighters of lake and stream that are now waiting for the disciples of Izaak Walton.

— FISHING IN CENTER OF SWIFT RIVER —

How to fish a rushing river in midstream successfully has been a mystery to many who have wanted to try their luck in the far-out pools that are difficult, if not impossible, to reach from shore. For such fishing, the board or trolling guide shown serves excellently.

The device is made from light pine and is 1½ ft. long, 6 in. wide, and ¾ in. thick. Both ends are pointed, as shown, the better to cut the water. Four screw eyes are driven into one side of the board. Wires that are stiff enough to prevent bending easily are attached to the eyes, as shown, by making a ring or eye at the ends. A horizontal wire with an eye at each end is run between the end wires and is attached to eyes made in the outer ends of the first wires. The line that runs to the boat or fisherman's rod

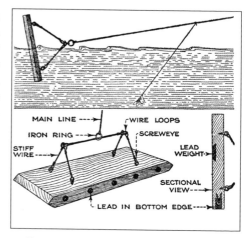

FISHING BLOCK OR TROLLING GUIDE FOR FISHING IN THE MIDDLE OF SWIFT CHANNEL.

has a ring fastened to it that slides freely along the crosswire. The line with the lure on it is connected to the main line, and with it one can reach the deep spots that cannot otherwise be successfully fished.

To make the block ride the water properly, the bottom edge must be ballasted with lead. Holes are drilled into the edge of the board with an auger bit, a staple or nail driven into the center of each hole, and melted lead is poured in. Enough holes are made and filled in this manner so that the block will be pulled down in the water to a depth of 3 in. Also, because there is a pull on the line side, this must be balanced by weighing down the opposite side. This can be done by cutting a dovetailed groove along the back of the board and filling it with melted lead, or by fastening a weight to the board above the center. This will make the device swim at the proper angle, so that when there is a pull on the line, the device will not turn over toward the line side.

— DRYING FISHING LINES —

Wet fishing lines rot rapidly; it is therefore not advisable to keep them on the reel, but they should be wound on a drier of some kind. A simple homemade one is shown in the illustration. It consists of a cylindrical paper box such as a large oatmeal box, glued onto an old

phonograph record as indicated. A tab with a ring in it is glued to the box at one end to provide a place to fasten the end of the line. Place the record on the phonograph and start the motor; this enables the line to be wound from the reel to the box in a very short time without any trouble.

— YARDSTICK FOR FISHING BOAT —

Fishing regulations are becoming more stringent every year, and the fisherman is kept busy with his ruler to avoid arrest for keeping fish that are under legal length. To simplify matters, some fishermen mark off the lengths of various kinds of fish on their rods. However, a simpler method of measuring the fish is to tack a yardstick along the inside of the boat, near the bottom, marking the length limit of each variety of fish on it. When a fish is caught, it is placed against the measure and it can be seen at a glance whether or not the fish may be kept.

— SPACED HOOKS ON TROTLINE ENGAGE TO AVOID ENTANGLING —

To keep hooks of a trotline from entangling when winding or unwinding it on a reel, one fisherman uses the following method: Space the staging lines so that the hooks at the end of each can be engaged as indicated.

— TWO KINKS FOR THE FISHERMAN —

TROT LINE

LINES SPACED SO THEY CAN BE HOOKED TOGETHER

The drawing shows a fish lure that seldom fails in its purpose, providing, of course, that there are fish in the vicinity. The lure consists of a transparent glass bowl, preferably a goldfish bowl about 6 or 8 in. in diameter, containing some minnows. It is suspended in the water a foot or two away from the point where the fisherman is fishing.

To make the lure, cut a circular piece of galvanized or copper screen wire, about 3/16-in. mesh to fit over the opening of the bowl. Solder four brass clips, shaped to fit under the edges of the bowl, to the screen as shown. These keep the screen firmly in place while the bowl is immersed. Wind two layers of friction tape around the neck of the bowl, coat well with a good varnish, and allow it to dry. Then take a line of 1/8-in. cotton, of sufficient length to go around the neck, and allow two suspension leads about 6 in. long. Form loops on the ends of the leads, and fasten the loops with common suspender clips. Then fasten the cord around the neck, apply another coat of varnish over the cord, allow it to dry, and the lure is ready for use. Fill the bowl with water and place some live minnows in it, put on the cover, and lower it into the water. Experience has shown that it is best to use from six to twelve minnows.

A fisherman employs this lure for catching herring and perch, with a minnow on his hook about 3 ft. away from the lure. When the water is clear, the fish can plainly be seen to dart at the minnows in the bowl. But, upon coming in contact with the glass, they seem to realize that something is wrong and immediately turn and snap at the minnow on the hook.

When removing fish from a stringer, it is usually necessary to force them back over the stringing needle, and this is not a very easy or pleasant task. To overcome this difficulty, use a detachable ring on the lower end of the stringer, as shown in the illustration. The ring is made of No. 8 galvanized wire with

the ends hooked to engage with each other, as indicated. By squeezing the ring, it is loosened and can be removed from the stringer. With one jerk of the stringer, the entire catch will slip off.

The stringing needle is made of the same size of wire as the ring. The stringer is made of braided cotton line of the desired length, the ends being looped and fastened with suspender clips.

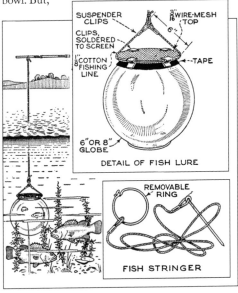

DETAIL OF FISH LURE

FISH STRINGER

ABOVE: A TRANSPARENT GLASS BOWL CONTAINING MINNOWS, WHICH FORMS AN EXCELLENT FISH LURE. BELOW: THE FISH STRINGER PROVIDED WITH DETACHABLE RING.

— REMOVING FISHHOOKS FROM CLOTHES —

To remove a fish-hook from your clothing without damaging the fabric, simply open the eye off the 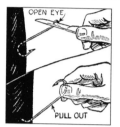 hook with a pocketknife and pull the shank through the cloth as indicated.

The REEL DEAL

— FISHING-ROD MAKING—
A ONE-PIECE CASTING ROD —

The pleasures of outdoor life are most keenly enjoyed by those sportsmen who are familiar with all the little tricks—the "ins and outs"—of the great wide open. It is the active participation in any chosen sport that makes the sport well worth while, for the enjoyment gleaned from little journeys to forest and stream largely rests with the sportsman's own knowledge of his sport. Not all of the fun of fishing lies in the catching of the fish, since the satisfaction that comes through handling a well-balanced rod and tackle must be reckoned the chief contributor to the outing. In other words, the pleasures of fishing do not depend so much upon the num-

ber of fish caught as the manner in which the person fishes for them.

The rod is naturally the first and most important consideration in the angler's kit, and it is the purpose of these articles to set forth, at first, a few hints that my own long experience leads me to think may be of some assistance to those anglers who enjoy making and repairing their own rods and tackle. This will be followed later by some suggestions on the art of angling generally. The hints given are merely my own methods, and while they may not be the best way of accomplishing the desired end, a good fishing rod may be constructed. Like the majority of amateurs I have achieved the desired results with a few common tools, namely, a saw, plane, jackknife, file, and sandpaper. These simple tools are all that is needed to turn out a serviceable and well-finished rod of excellent action.

— KIND OF MATERIAL —

The great elasticity and durability of the split-cane or split-bamboo rod cannot be easily disputed. The handmade split bamboo is unquestionably the best rod for every kind of fishing, but it is also the most expensive and the most difficult material for the amateur to work. In making the first rod or two, the beginner will be better satisfied with the results in making a good solid-wood rod. Of course, glued-up split bamboo butts, joints, and tip stock may be purchased, and if the angler is determined to have only bamboo, it is advisable to purchase these built-up sections rather than to risk certain failure by attempting to glue the cane. However, there are several good woods particularly well adapted for rod making. And though slightly inferior to the finest bamboo in elasticity and spring, the carefully made solid-wood rod is good enough for any angler and will probably suit the average fisherman as well as any rod that can be purchased.

Bethabara, or washaba, a native wood of British Guinea, makes a fine rod but it is a heavy wood, very hard, and for this reason is perhaps less desirable than all other woods. With the single exception of snakewood, it is the heaviest wood for rod making and is only used for short bait-casting rods. Possessing considerable strength, bethabara can be worked quite slender, and a 5-ft. casting tip can be safely made of 5-oz. weight.

Greenheart, a South American wood, is popular with manufacturers and amateur rod makers alike, and 90 percent of the better class of solid-wood rods are made of this material. It resembles bethabara in color, but is lighter in weight, although it apparently possesses about the same strength and elasticity. In point of fact, there is little, if any, difference between the woods. Providing sound and well-selected wood is used, the merits of a rod made of bethabara or greenheart are more likely to be due to the careful workmanship of the maker than to the variety of the wood used.

Dagame, or dagama, a native of the forests of Cuba, is in many respects the ideal material for rod making because it has strength and elasticity. This wood is straight-grained and free from knots, which makes it easily worked. It polishes well and is durable. While there is always more or less difficulty about procuring first-class bethabara and greenheart, dagame of good quality is easily obtained.

Lancewood is much used in turning out the cheaper grades of fishing rods, but it is somewhat soft and has a marked tendency to take set under the strain of fishing and warp out of shape. It is less expensive than the other woods, and while it has a straight and even grain, there are numerous small knots present that make this material less satisfactory to work than the other woods. For heavy sea rods, lancewood may serve the purpose fairly well, but for the smaller fishing tools this material is inferior to bethabara, greenheart, and dagame. Other woods are often used, and while a good rod may be frequently made from almost any of them, the three mentioned are held in the highest esteem by the angling fraternity. For the first rod, the amateur will make no mistake in selecting dagame, whether the slender fly rod or the more easily constructed short bait-casting tool is to be made.

— THE NECESSARY TOOLS —

The construction of a thoroughly well-made and nicely balanced rod is more a matter of careful work than outfit, but a few suitable tools will greatly facilitate the labor. A good firm workbench or table 4 ft. or more in length will be needed. A regulation bench vise will come in handy, but one of the small iron vises will do very well. A couple of iron planes, one of medium size for rough planing work, and a small 4-in. block plane for finishing will be required. As the cutters of the planes must be kept as sharp as possible to do good work, a small oilstone—preferably one in a wood case with cover to keep out dust—will be needed. You'll also need a coarse single-cut mill file about 16 in. long, a few sheets of No. 1 and No. 0 sandpaper, a sheet or two of fine emery cloth, a small thin "back" or other saw, and a steel cabinet scraper.

A caliper of some kind is a necessity, and while the best is a micrometer, *Figure 1,* registering to a thousandth part of an inch as well as indicating 8ths, 16ths, 32ds, and 64ths, this tool is somewhat expensive. But a very good caliper may be had in the sliding–arm type, *Figure 2,* with the scale graduated to 64ths and taking work up to 2 in. in diameter.

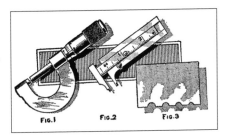

TWO TOOLS FOR GAUGING THE DIAMETER OF THE RODS, AND A HOMEMADE SCRAPER.

Cheaper measuring gauges are to be had in plenty, but as the brass and boxwood scales are provided only with coarse graduations, the better quality of mechanics' tools will give better satisfaction.

The grooved planes used by the professional rod makers are rather expensive, although they are most convenient for quickly rounding up the rod to the desired diameter. However, the beginner may dispense with the planes by making the tool illustrated in *Figure 3.* To make this handy little tool, purchase a steel wood scraper such as cabinetmakers use, and file a series of grooves along the edges with round file. File at right angles to the steel, finishing up with a fine file to give a sharp cutting edge. The tool thus made is very handy for scraping the rod after it has been roughly rounded with the plane. Its use will be mentioned later on in the description.

— FIVE-FOOT BAITCASTING ROD —

The short one-piece baitcasting rod with but one ferrule is the easiest rod to make, and for this reason the beginner will do well to select this popular type for the first attempt. As the total length of the rod is to measure 5 ft. exclusive of the agate tip, the wood should be 1 or 2 in. longer to allow for cutting down to 60 in.

Having selected a good strip of dagame ⅝ in. square, run the plane along each side and from both ends. This will determine the direction in

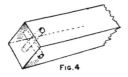

FIG. 4

which the grain runs. Drill two holes at the end decided upon for the butt, spacing them about ¼ in. from the end as shown in *Figure 4*. Drive a stout brad into the corner of the bench top and hook the butt end over the nail. By rigging the stick up in this manner it will be securely held, and planing may be done with the grain with greater ease and accuracy than when the end of the stick is butted up against a cleat nailed to the bench top.

The wood should be planed straight and true from end to end and calipered until it is ½ in. square. It may appear crooked, but this need not trouble one at this stage of the work, because it may be made perfectly straight later on. Overlook any kinks and do not attempt to straighten the stick by planing more from one side than the other. The chief thing to be done is to fashion a square stick, and when the caliper shows the approximate diameter draw cross lines at the ends to find the center.

The length of the hand grasp should be marked out. If a double grasp is wanted, allow 12 in. from the butt end. This will afford an 11-in. hand grasp after sawing off the end in which the holes were drilled. For a single hand grasp make an allowance of 11 in. However, the double grasp—with cork above and below the reel seat—is preferred by most anglers because it affords a better grip for the hand when reeling in the line. Mark the hand-grasp distance by running a knife mark around the rod 12 in. from the butt end.

Lay out a diagram showing the full length of the rod by placing a strip of paper—the unprinted back of a strip of wallpaper is just the thing—on the bench and drawing two lines from the diameter of the butt to that of the tip. Although the caliber of casting rods differs somewhat, the dimensions given will suit the average angler and I would advise the beginner to make the rod to these measurements. For the butt, draw a line exactly ½ in. long across the paper, and from the center of this line run a straight pencil mark at right angles to the tip end, or 60 in. distant, at which point another cross line is drawn, exactly ⅛ in. long, to represent the diameter. Connect the ends of these two cross lines to make

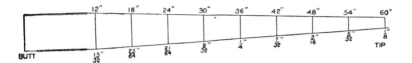

FIG. 5 DIAGRAM OR LAYOUT FOR A ONE-PIECE BAITCASTING ROD, SHOW-
ING CALLIPERED DIMENSIONS FOR EACH SIX INCHES OF LENGTH. A PAPER
PATTERN OF ANY ROD MAY BE DRAWN UP, PROVIDING THE AMATEUR ROD
MAKER HAS A ROD TO USE FOR A PATTERN, OR POSSESSES THE EXACT
DIAMETER OF THE ROD AT INTERVALS OF SIX INCHES ALONG ITS LENGTH.

a long tapering form. Divide this pattern into eight equal parts, beginning at 12 in. from the butt end, marking a cross-link at every 6 in. This layout is shown exaggerated in *Figure 5.* If it is desired to copy a certain rod, find the diameter at the several 6-in. stations with the caliper and write them down at the corresponding sections of the paper diagram. However, if a splendid all-around casting rod is desired, it is perfectly safe to follow the dimensions given in *Figure 5,* which show the manner of dividing the paper pattern into the equal parts and the final diameter of the rod at each 6-in. station, or line.

Procure a small strip of thin brass, or zinc, and file nine slots on one edge to correspond in diameter with the width of the

horizontal lines that indicate the diameter of the rod on the pattern. This piece is shown in *Figure 6.* By making use of the pattern and the brass gauge, the rod may be given the desired taper and the work will proceed more quickly than if the caliper is alone relied upon to repeatedly check up the work.

When a good layout of the work is thus made, the next step is to carefully plane the stick so that it will be evenly tapered in the square. Plane with the grain and from the butt toward the tip end, and make frequent tests with caliper and gauge, noting the diameter every 6 in. Mark all the thick spots with a pencil and

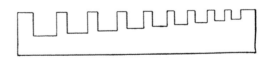

FIG. 6 GAUGE MADE OF SHEET BRASS WITH SLOTS
CORRESPONDING IN LENGTH AND WIDTH TO
THE CALIPER-LAYOUT MEASUREMENTS.

plane lightly to reduce the wood to the proper diameter. Reduce the stick in this manner until all sides have an even taper from the butt to the tip. The stick should now be perfectly square with a nice, even taper. Test it by resting the tip end on the floor and bending it from the butt end. Note the arch it takes and see if it resumes its original shape when the pressure is released. If it does, the elasticity of the material is as is should be. But if it remains bent or takes "set," the wood is very likely imperfectly seasoned and the rod should be hung up in a warm closet, or near the kitchen stove for a few weeks to season.

To facilitate the work of planing the stick to shape, a length of pine board with a groove in one edge will be found handy. A 5-ft. length of the ordinary tongue-and-groove board, about 1 in. thick, will be just the thing. As the tip of the rod is smaller than the butt, plane the groove in the board to make it gradually shallower to correspond to the taper of the rod. Nail this board, with the groove uppermost, to the edge of the workbench and place the rod in the groove with one of the square corners up, which can be easily taken off with the finely set plane. Plane off

the other three corners in a like manner, transforming the square stick into one of octagonal form. This part of the work should be carefully done, and the stick frequently calipered at each 6-in. mark, to obtain the proper taper.

It is important to make each of the eight sides as nearly uniform as the caliper and eye can do it. Set the cutter of the small plane very fine, lay the strip in the groove and plane off the corner the full length of the stick, then turn another corner uppermost and plane it off, and so on, until the stick is almost round and tapering gradually from the mark of the hand grasp to the tip.

To make the rod perfectly round, use the steel scraper in which the grooves were filed and scrape the whole rod to remove any flat or uneven spots. Finish by sandpapering smooth.

The action of the rod differs with the material used. In trying out the action it is wise to tie on the tip and guides and affix the reel by a string in order to try a few casts. If the action seems about right, give the rod a final smoothing with No. 0 sandpaper.

For the hand grasp nothing is so good as solid cork, and while hand

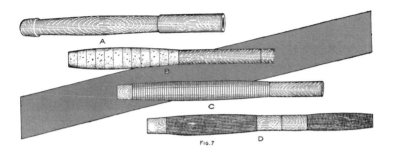

FIG.7

THE FOUR DIFFERENT TYPES OF HAND GRASPS ARE A WOOD SLEEVE BORED TO FIT THE BUTT OF THE ROD; THE BUILT-UP CORK OVER A WOOD SLEEVE; A CANE-WOUND GRASP; AND THE DOUBLE CORD-WOUND GRASPS WITH A REEL SEAT BETWEEN THEM.

grasps may be purchased assembled, it is a simple matter to make them. In *Figure 7* are shown four kinds of handles, namely, a wood sleeve or core, *A*, bored to fit the butt of the rod and shaped for winding the fishing cord; a built-up cork grasp, *B*, made by cementing cork washers over a wood sleeve or directly to the butt of the rod; a can-wound grip, *C*, most used for saltwater fishing; and the double-wound grip, *D*, made in one piece, then sawn apart in the center, the forward grip being glued into place after the reel seat is in position.

To make a grip, select a number of cork washers, which may be obtained from dealers in the wholesale drug trade or from any large fishing-tackle dealer. Make a tool for cutting a hole in their centers from a piece of tubing or an old ferrule of the required diameter by filing one edge sharp, then covering the other end with several thicknesses of cloth. Turn this tube around in the cork like a wad cutter. If the cutter is sharp, a nice clean cut will result, but the opposite will likely occur if an attempt is made to hammer the tube through the cork.

Having cut the butt end of the rod off square about 1 in. from the end, or enough to remove the holes, smear a little hot glue on the end, drop a cork washer over the tip of the rod, and work it down to the

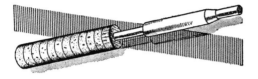

FIG. 8 THE CORKS GLUED IN PLACE ON THE
BUTT AND THE WOOD SLEEVE, OR REEL-
SEAT CORE, READY TO SLIDE DOWN
AND GLUE IN POSITION.

butt. Cut another cork, give the first one a coat of glue, slip the former over the tip, and press the two together. Proceed until about 10 corks have been glued together in position. This will make a hand grasp a trifle over 5 in. long.

A sleeve will be needed for the reel seat to slip over, and a soft-wood core of this sort can be purchased from any dealer in rod-making materials, or it can be made at home. For the material, procure a piece of white pine about ¾ in. in diameter and 5 in. long. A section sawn from a discarded curtain roller will serve the purpose well. Bore a $^{15}/_{32}$-in. hole through the piece and plane down the outside until it slips inside the reel seat. It should be well made and a good fit, and one end tapered to fit the taper of the reel seat while the opposite end should be about ¼ in.

shorter than the reel seat. Slide this wood sleeve down the rod, as shown in *Figure 8*, coat the rod and the upper part of the last cork with glue and force the sleeve tightly in place. A day or two should be allowed for the glue to set and thoroughly dry before giving the hand grasp the final touches.

If a lathe is at hand, the hand grasp may be turned to any desired shape. But most anglers prefer a cylindrical-shaped grip, leaving the top cork untrimmed to form a kind of shoulder when the metal reel seat is pressed into the cork. If corks of 1¼-in diameter are purchased, little trimming will be necessary to work the hand grasp down to 1¹/₁₆ in. in diameter. This size seems to fit the average hand about right. The lower corks will need a little trimming to fit the taper of the butt cap so that it may fit snugly in place. Cement the butt cap in place by heating the cap moderately hot, then rub a little of the melted ferrule cement inside the cap and force it over the cork butt. When the cement has hardened, drive a small brass pin or brad through the cap and file the ends off flush with the metal surface. All the guides, ferrules, and reel seat are shown in *Figure 9*.

The regulation metal reel seat is about 4½ in. long, and in fitting it to the old type of bait rod the covered hood is affixed to the upper end of the reel seat. This arrangement is satisfactory enough for the 9-ft. bait rod, but it is rather awkward in fitting it to the short baitcasting rod, as with the hood at the upper end the reel is pushed so far forward that it leaves 1 in. or more of the reel seat exposed, and the hand must grip this smooth metal instead of the cork.

To avoid this, it is best to cut the reel seat to the rod with the hood at the lower end near the hand. For a single hand grasp, a tapered winding check will be needed to make a neat finish and this should be ordered of the correct diameter to fit the reel seat at the lower end and the diameter of the rod at the other. In the double hand grasp the winding check is used to finish off the upper end of the cork, which is tapering to fit the rod at this point.

In assembling the reel seat, push it with the hooded end well down and work it into the cork to make a tight waterproof joint. Push the reel seat up the rod, coat the sleeve with cement and push the reel seat home.

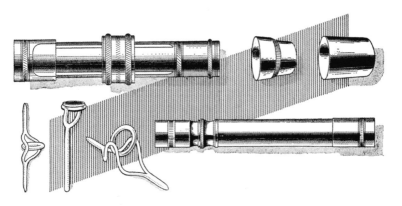

FIG. 9 THE MOUNTINGS USED ON A BAITCASTING ROD CONSIST OF A REEL SEAT, BUTT CAP, TAPER SLEEVE, NARROW AGATE GUIDE, AGATE OFFSET TOP, ONE RING GUIDE, AND A WELTED, SHOULDERED FERRULE.

Drive a small pin through the hooded end and reel seat to make the whole rigid. This pin should not be drive through the rod or it will weaken it at this point. Just let it enter the wood a short distance to prevent the reel seat from turning.

The upper or double grasp is fashioned after the reel seat is in position, and the corks are cemented on and pushed tightly together in the same manner as used in forming the lower grasp. The first cork should be pressed tightly against the upper end of the reel seat and turned about so that the metal may enter the cork and form a tight joint. As many corks as are required to form a grip of proper length are in turn cemented to each other and the rod. After the glue has become dry, the cork may be worked down and tapered to make a smooth swelled grasp. The winding check is now cemented on, to make a neat finish between the upper grip and the rod.

Before affixing the guides, go over the rod with fine sandpaper, then wet the wood to raise the grain and repeat this operation using old sandpaper. If an extra-fine polish is wanted, rub it down with powdered pumice and oil, or rottenstone and oil, and finish off with an oiled rag.

To fit the agate tip, file down the end of the rod with a fine-cut file until it is a good fit in the metal tube. Melt a little of the ferrule cement and smear a little on the tip of the rod, then push the agate down in place.

Spar varnish is often used to protect the rod, but extra-light coach varnish gives a better gloss, and it is as durable and waterproof as any varnish. It is necessary to purchase only a quarter pint of the varnish, because a very small quantity is used. The final varnishing is, of course, done after the rod has been wound and the guides are permanently whipped into position. However, it is an excellent idea to fill the pores of the wood by rubbing it with a cloth saturated in the varnish before the silk whippings are put on. Merely fill the cells of the wood and wipe off all surplus, leaving the rod clean and smooth.

The guides may now be fastened in place, and for the 5-ft. rod, only two of them are necessary. The first guide should be placed 19½ in. from the metal taper, which finishes off the upper hand grasp, and the second guide spaced 15½ in. from the first. By spacing the guides in this manner, the line will run through them with the least possible friction.

— Winding, or Whipping, the Rod —

Before whipping on the guides, take a fine file and round off the sharp edges of the base to prevent the possibility of the silk being cut. Measure off the required distances at which the guides are to be affixed and fasten them in position by winding with a few turns of common thread. Ordinary silk of No. A size may be used, but No. 00 is the best for small rods. Most anglers agree that the size of the silk to use for the whippings should be in proportion to the size of the rod—heavy silk for the heavy rod, and a fine silk for the small rod. Size A is the finest silk commonly stocked in stores, but one or more spools of No. 00 and No. 0 may be ordered from any large dealer in fishing tackle. As a rule, size 0 gives a more workmanlike finish to the butt and joints of fly and bait rods, while No. 00 is about right to use for winding the tips. In fact, all rods weighing up to 6 oz. may be whipped with No. 00 size.

In whipping the rod, the so-called invisible knot is used. Begin the whipping as shown in *E, Figure 10*, by tucking the end under the first coil and holding it with the left thumb. The spool of silk is held in the right hand and the rod is turned to the left, sufficient tension being kept on the silk so that it can be evenly coiled with each strand tightly against the other. A loop of silk, some 4 in. long, is well waxed and placed so that its end will project a short distance beyond the last coil, which finishes the whipping. This detail is shown in *F*. In whipping on guides, begin the whipping at the base and work over the pointed end

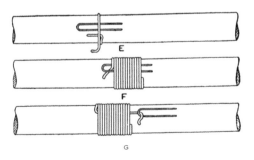

of the flange, winding on sufficient silk to extend about ⅛ in. beyond the pointed flange of the guide base. When the last coil is made, cut off the thread from the spool and tuck the end under the whipping by pulling on the ends of the waxed loop, as shown in G. Cut off the ends neatly with a sharp knife.

For colors, bright red and a medium shade of apple green are the best because these colors keep their original tint after varnishing and are less likely to fade than the more delicate shades. Red finished off with a narrow circle of green always looks good, and red with yellow is likewise a good combination. Narrow windings look much better than wide whippings, and a dozen turns make about as wide a winding as the angler desires. For edgings, three or four turns of silk are about right, and these should be put on after the wider windings have been whipped on and in the same manner, although it is best to tuck the ends of the edging beneath the wider winding when pulling the end through to make the invisible knot.

— VARNISHING THE ROD —

After winding the rod, see that all fuzzy ends are neatly clipped off, then go over the silk windings with a coat of shellac. The shellac can be made by dissolving a little white shellac in grain alcohol. Warm the shellac and apply it with a small camel's-hair brush, giving the silk only two light coats. Allow the rod to stand a couple of days for the shellac to become thoroughly dry.

A small camel's-hair brush will be required for the varnishing—one about ½ in. wide will do. If the varnishing is to be done out of doors, a clear and warm day should be selected and the can of coach varnish should be placed in a pot of hot water for five minutes so that the varnish will spread evenly. A temperature of about 75 degrees is best for this work, because the varnish will not spread if cold or in a cold place. The varnish should be evenly brushed on, and care taken that no spots are left untouched. Hang up by the tip to dry in a room free from dust. Although the varnish will set in four or five hours, it is a good plan to allow three days for drying between coats. Two coats will suffice to protect the rod, but as properly applied coach varnish is rather thin in body, three coats will give complete protections to the wood.

The materials for this rod are:

1 dagame or greenheart stick,
    5 ft. long and $5/8$ in. square;
1 reel seat with straight hood,
    $3/4$ in.;
1 butt cap, 1 in.;

1 taper, small end $15/32$ in.;
1 offset, or angle, agate top, $3/32$
    in.; and
2 narrow agate guides, $1/2$ in., all
    in German silver;
2 dozen corks, $1\frac{1}{4}$ by $1\frac{1}{8}$ in.;
    and
two 50-yd. spools of silk, red
    and green, 00 size.

— Various Two- and Three-piece Rods —

Although the action of the one-piece rod is undeniably better than when the rod is made in two or three pieces, it is less compact to carry. To make a 5-ft., two-piece baitcasting rod, the same dimensions as given for the one-piece rod will make a very fine fishing tool. It is wise to make two tips in view of a possible breakage. The rod may consist of two pieces of equal length, but a rod of better action is secured by making the butt section somewhat shorter with a relatively longer tip. By making the butt section about 23 in. long, exclusive of ferrule and butt cap, and the tip section $32\frac{1}{2}$ in. long, a splendid little rod is obtained that will fit any of the regulation rod cases of 35-in. length. To make a $6\frac{1}{2}$-oz. rod of this kind with a cork hand grasp, caliper it in the same

manner as the one-piece rod, making the butt section $32\frac{1}{2}$ in. long, tapering from $15/32$ in. at the upper end of the hand grasp to $19/64$ in. at the ferrule. The tip is made 33 in. long, tapering from $17/64$ in. to $7/64$ in. By making the tip and butt to these lengths both parts will be of equal length when the ferrules and the tops are added.

The material list is as follows, the attachments being made of German silver: dagame or greenheart butt, $5/8$ in. by 3 ft. long; two tips $3/8$ in. by 3 ft. long; one $3/4$-in. reel seat with straight hood; one 1-in. butt cap; one taper, $15/32$ in. at the small end; two $3/32$-in. offset agate tops; two $1/2$-in. narrow agate guides; two No. 1 size one-ring casting guides; one $17/64$-in. welted and shouldered ferrule with two closed-end centers,

THE MAKING OF A ROD NOT ONLY AFFORDS MUCH PLEASURE
BUT THE ROD CAN BE CONSTRUCTED AS DESIRED.

one for each tip; two dozen cork washers, 1¼ in. in diameter, and two spools of winding silk.

The three-piece rod should be made up to 6 ft. in length to secure the best action, but even if so made, the use of the extra ferrules makes the rod less resilient and elastic than the rod of one- or two-piece construction. The best action is obtained only when the rod bends to a uniform curve, and because the ferrules cannot conform to this curve or arc, the more joints incorporated in a rod, the less satisfactory it will be from an angling standpoint. Convenience in packing and carrying are the sole merits that the many-jointed rod possesses.

Complete specifications for making a three-piece baitcasting rod, together with a material list, is as follows: A rod, about 5½ ft. long with a single or double hand grasp made of cork, will weigh about 7 oz. Caliper the butt so that it will taper from 15/32 in. to 11/32 in. at the cap of the ferrule, making it 21½ in. long. The middle joint is tapered from 21/64 in. to 15/64 in., and is 21¾ in. long; the tips are 21 in. long and are tapered from 13/64 in. to 7/64 in. Dagame or greenheart is used for the butt, joint, and tips, and German silver for the fittings. All pieces are 2 ft. long, the butt is 5/8 in., the joint and tips, 3/8 in.; one 3/4-in. reel seat with straight hood; one 1-in. butt cap; one taper, small end 15/32 in.; one 21/64-in. welted and shouldered ferrule; one 15/64-in. welted and shouldered ferrule with two closed centers, one for each tip; two 3/32-in. offset agate tops; two ½-in. narrow agate guides; two No. 1 size one-ring casting guides; two dozen cork washers, and winding silk, size 00 or 0.

— FLY RODS FOR TROUT AND BASS —

Having made a good baitcasting rod, the amateur will find little trouble in making a rod with a number of joints. No special instructions need be given because the work of planing and smoothing up the wood, and finishing and mounting the rod, is the same as has been described in detail before.

For fly-fishing for trout, accuracy and delicacy are of more importance than length of cast. The rod best suited to this phase of angling differs greatly from that used in baitcasting. A stiff, heavy rod is entirely unsuited for fly casting and while it is, of course, possible to make a rod too willowy for the sport, the amateur, working by rule of thumb, is more likely to err on the other side and make the fly rods of too stout a caliber. The idea is simply to help the amateur over the hard part by giving a list of dimensions of a representative trout and a bass fly rod.

To make a 9-ft. trout fly rod, with a cork grasp having a length of 9 in. above the reel seat, caliper the material as follows: The butt is tapered from 7/16 in. to 25/64 in. at 1 ft. from the butt end; 1½ ft., 11/32 in.; 2 ft., 21/64 in.; 2½ ft., 5/16 in.; and 3 ft., 19/64 in. The first 6 in. of the middle joint is calipered to 9/32 in.; 1 ft., 17/64 in.; 1½ ft., 15/64 in.; 2 ft., 7/32 in.; 2½ ft., 13/64 in.; and 3 ft., 3/16 in. The first 6 in. of the tips are calipered to 11/64 in.; 1 ft., 5/32 in.; 1½ ft., ⅛ in.; 2 ft., 7/64 in.; 2½ ft., 3/32 in.; and 3 ft., 5/64 in. All joints are made 36½ in.

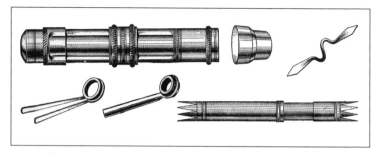

THE MOUNTINGS FOR A FLY ROD CONSIST OF A REEL SEAT WITH A STRAIGHT HOOD, A TAPER, SNAKE GUIDE, AGATE ANGLE TOP, AND SERRATED FERRULE. THE TOOTHED ENDS ARE WOUND WITH SILK TO AFFORD ADDITIONAL STRENGTH.

long. The material used is dagame or greenheart the butt being ⅝ in. by 4 ft., the joint ⅜ in. by 4 ft., and the tips ⅜ in. by 4 ft. The attachments of German silver are: one ¾-in. reel seat, fly-rod type with butt cap; one taper, 3 ¾₆₄ in. at the small end; one ⁹/₃₂-in. welted and shouldered ferrule; one ¹¹/₆₄-in. welted and shouldered ferrule with two closed-end centers, one for each tip; two No. 4 snake guides for the middle joint, and six No. 2 snake guides, three for each tip section; two No. 7 agate angle fly tops, the kind to wind on; one dozen cork washers, and two 10-yd. spools of winding silk 00 size.

A bass fly rod 9½ ft. long, weighing 7½ oz., with a cork grasp 9½ in. above the reel seat, is calipered as follows: The butt is tapered from ¹³/₃₂ in. to ²⁵/₆₄ in. 1 ft. from the end; 1½ ft. from butt, ²³/₆₄ in.; 2 ft., ¹¹/₃₂ in.; 2½ ft., ²¹/₆₄ in.; and 3 ft., ¹⁹/₆₄ in. The first 6 in. of the middle joint is ¹⁹/₆₄ in.; 1 ft., ⁹/₃₂ in.; 1½ ft., ¹⁷/₆₄ in.; 2 ft., ¹⁵/₆₄ in.; 2½ ft., ⁷/₃₂ in.; and 3 ft., ¹³/₆₄ in. The first 6 in. of the tips, ¹¹/₆₄ in.; 1 ft., ⁵/₃₂ in.; 1 ½ ft., ⁹/₆₄ in.; 2 ft., ⅛ in.; 2½ ft., ⁷/₆₄ in.; and 3 ft., ⁵/₆₄ in. The joints are 36½ in. long. The mountings are the same as for the trout fly rod. Dagame or greenheart wood is used, the butt being ⅝ in. by 4 ft., the joint ⅜ in. by 4 ft., and the tips ⅜ in. by 4 ft.

The two-piece saltwater rod with an 18-in. double cork hand grasp, the whole being 6½ ft. long, is made to weight about 13 oz., with the following caliperings: A uniform taper of ³⁵/₆₄ in. to ²⁹/₆₄ in., from the cork grasp to the ferrule, is given to the butt. The first 6 in. of the tips is $13/32$ in.; 1 ft., $25/64$ in.; 1½ ft., $11/32$ in.; 2 ft., $21/64$ in.; 2½ ft., $9/32$ in., and to tip, $15/64$ in. The joints are made 36¾ in. long. Dagame or greenheart is used with German silver mountings. Both pieces of wood are 4 ft. long,

the butt being of ¾-in. and the tip of ½-in. material. One ⅞-in. reel seat with straight hood, one 1-in. butt cap, one $7/16$-in. ferrule, one taper with small end $35/64$ in.; one $10/32$-in. stirrup-tube agate top; two No. 3 bell guides; two dozen cork washers, and two spools, size A, winding silk.

— THE INDEPENDENT-BUTT ROD —

The independent-butt rod in which the hand grasp contains the ferrule and the tip is made in one piece, is a favorite type with many of the best fishermen. This mode of construction may be used with all classes of rods, the light fly- and baitcasting rods, and the heavier caliber rods used in saltwater angling. In rods of this type, it is necessary to use the same size ferrule to make as many tips as desired to fit the one butt. Tips of several calibers and weights may thus be fashioned to fit the one butt, and if the single-piece tip is too long for some special use, one tip may be made a jointed one for ease in carrying.

The independent butt or hand grasp is made by fitting the ferrule directly on a length of dagame or greenheart that has been rounded so that the seated ferrule will not touch

the wood. The ferrule is then cemented and riveted in place, and a soft-pine sleeve is fitted over the wood core and the ferrule. The forward end of the sleeve is, of course, tapered to fit the taper of the reel seat. When properly fitted, its lower end will project about ¼ in. beyond the pine sleeve. Glue the sleeve on this wood core, cement the reel seat to the sleeve, and rivet the reel seat in place.

The cork washers are glued in position, working the first one into the metal edge of the reel seat to make a nice tight joint at this point. The other corks are then glued in place until the hand grasp is of the desired length. The projecting end of the wood core is then cut off flush with the last cork and the rod is mounted in the usual manner.

In making a double hand grasp,

the forward grasp may be fitted over the wood core in the fashion already described in making the hand grasp for the one-piece baitcasting rod. Or the forward grasp may be fitted to the tip, just above the ferrule, as preferred. Both methods are commonly used, the only difference being in the manner of finishing the forward grasp. If the forward grip is affixed to the ferruled end of the tip, two tapered thimbles will be required to make a nice finish.

The heavy-surf, or tarpon, rod is made up of an independent, detachable butt 20 in. long, having a solid-cork or cord-wound hand grasp, and a one-piece tip, 5½ ft. long. It should weigh altogether 23½ oz. It is uniformly calipered to taper from $29/32$ in. to $5/16$ in. One piece of dagame or greenheart, 1 in. by 6½ ft., will be required as well as one 1-in. reel seat for detachable butt, including one ¾-in. male ferrule; one 1⅛-in. butt cap; two No. 11 wide, raised agate guides; two No. 1 trumpet guides; one ⅜-in. agate stirrup top; two spools of winding silk, A-size, and two dozen cork washers, or sufficient fish line to cord the butt. The guides are whipped on double, the first set spaced 10 in. from the top and the second, 26 in. from the reel. The core of the independent or detachable butt is constructed of the same material as the rod, which makes the hand grasp somewhat elastic and very much superior to a stiff and rigid butt.

— REPAIRING A FISHING ROD —

Many a broken fishing rod is laid aside because the owner does not know how to repair it properly. The ordinary method of repair is to cut the two ends at an angle and, after applying glue to the surfaces,

JOINT

DARNING NEEDLE

to join them and wind silk around the joint.

This method can be greatly improved upon by reinforcing the splice with a medium-size darning needle. The sharp end is driven into one piece and the other end is then ground to a point and pushed into the other piece. It may be necessary to drill a small hole in the second piece with a fine drill in order to force the ground point into it without pushing the needle down farther in the first one. The joint, of course, is glued and wound with silk in the usual way. A splice thus made will be the strongest part of the whole rod.

— A Homemade Fishing Float Adjustable to Depth —

A novel device for fishing, especially with a short baitcasting rod, is a float that can be adjusted to the depth of water in which it is desired to fish. The float is hollow and slides on the line. To use it, the casting lead and hooks are adjusted as usual, and a sliding knot on the line is set for the depth desired, and the cast made. The float will stop at the sliding knot and remain on the surface. In reeling the line, the knot passes freely through the guides and the float slides down the line until it reaches the casting weight.

Cork is a good material from which to make the float. Cut the cork in sections, as shown, and fit it over a large quill, which provides a smooth-running hole through the float. Fit a small glass bead in the upper end of the float as a stop for the knot. The knot is of the figure-eight type, and tied as shown. It slides easily but grips the line tightly enough to stop the float. An ordinary float can be altered for use as described.

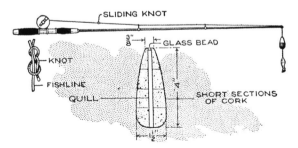

BY SETTING A SLIDING KNOT ON THE LINE, AS A STOP FOR THE FLOAT, THE DEPTH AT WHICH THE SINKER IS DESIRED CAN BE EASILY REGULATED.

— STEEL-TUBE CASE FOR FISHING ROD —

Fishing rods of the one-piece type may be protected against rough handling by inserting them into a length of thin-wall steel tubing. These are cut to the required length and both ends are closed with rubber crutch tips, which may be purchased at a dime store.

STEEL TUBING

CRUTCH TIPS

FISHING ROD

— MAKING ROUND RODS FOR FISHING POLES —

In looking forward to the enjoyment that may be had in the spring, it is good to prepare and overhaul the fishing apparatus or the shooting equipment. In doing so, it may be necessary to make a joint for the fishing rod or perhaps a rod for the gun. These can be easily cut if they are sized and run through holes made in a piece of thin metal as follows: Make several holes of the desired sizes in a steel plate and ream them out with a rather dull taper reamer, so as to leave a burr on one side. This burr should be filed down almost level with the surface of the metal, leaving the edges flat and sharp. If a rod of wood from which the article is to be made is put in a hole and drawn through from the opposite side to the burr, a nice round rod will result. As the rod becomes smaller, use a smaller hole until the required diameter is obtained. A saw plate that is not too thin is the proper thing to use for the steel plate. It will be necessary to draw the temper to make the holes, but it is not necessary to retemper it after the holes are made.

— LOOP IN END OF LINE TO CHANGE FISHHOOKS EASILY —

When it is necessary to change hooks or plugs frequently while fishing, the following kink will save time: Double the line at the end and tie it in a knot, forming a loop large enough for the hook or plug to slip through. Then thread the loop through the eye of a hook, pass the hook through the loop as indicated, and draw the line tightly.

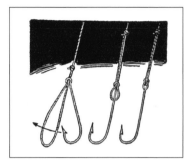

— FISHING ROD WRAPPED WITH AID OF A PENCIL AND ERASER —

To apply a tight, smooth wrapping of thread when making repairs on a split-bamboo fishing rod, one angler suggests the use of a pencil and eraser. The pencil carries the spool of thread so that it may be rotated easily around the rod, and the eraser is slit to receive the thread and hold it tightly during the operation.

— CORK PROTECTS CASTING-ROD TIP AND HOLDS HOOK SAFELY —

Accidental breakage of the agate tip in a casting rod is prevented by inserting a tiny cork inside the guide as shown. The hook is also shielded by sticking it in the cork to cover the barbed end.

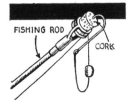

TERRIFIC TACKLE BOX

— A FISHING-TACKLE OUTFIT
IN A SHOTGUN SHELL —

At the camp or on the trail, an emergency fishing-tackle outfit is almost as handy as matches, compass, and knife, and it may be the means of saving one's life. A convenient way to carry such an outfit is in two old shotgun shells, telescoped.

The hooks, on a cork, and the sinkers are fitted snugly into the shell. Several yards of line are then wound on the outside. This outfit can be stowed in a pocket handily, always ready for use.

— SHOTGUN SHELL HOLDS PARAFFIN
TO WAX FISHLINE —

A handy method of waxing your fishline to preserve it is to carry a discharged shotgun shell that been filled with melted paraffin. A deep slot in the end of the shell permits the line to be drawn over the wax quickly.

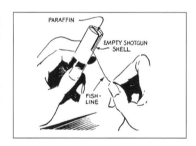

— SAFETY PIN HOLDS FISHHOOKS —

Fishhooks can be kept from getting tangled and scattered around by just stringing them on a safety pin. Pins of various sizes may  be used in proportion to the number and size of hooks carried, which can be taken off one at a time as they are needed.

— Camper's Bait Cache —

Campers desiring a sure supply of angleworms for fishing will find the bait cache shown in the sketch convenient and practical. A box, about 18 in. long and 10 in. square on the end, is stuck into the ground in a shady place, and all the bait dug by the campers on their arrival is placed into it. The soil used to fill the box should be rich black loam, quite moist but wet enough to be sticky. A few inches of the top of the box is left unfilled and a double layer of green sod is fitted over it, as shown in the sectional view. The upper sod is arranged level with the surface of the ground and should be cut carefully so that it will not be observed by prowlers. If the region where fishing is to be done is such that angleworms cannot be obtained easily, it is best to dig them before starting for camp. The bait cache may then be made as a convenient place in which to keep the bait in good condition for fishing.

ANGLEWORMS FOR FISHING BAIT MAY BE KEPT SATISFACTORILY IN THE BURIED BOX COVERED WITH SOD.

SOD
SOD
MOIST DIRT

— BOX FOR LIVE BAIT IN ROWBOAT IS UNDER HINGED SEAT —

Two watertight bulkheads under the middle seat, and holes bored in the bottom, provide a bait well where the water is always cool and fresh. Paint with oil paint and linseed oil and caulk the joints with marine glue.

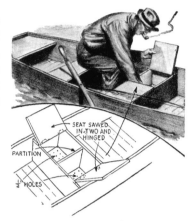

— WATERPROOF FISHHOOK HOLDER —

A piece of clear sheet celluloid rolled to form a cylinder and cemented together with acetone provides a handy holder for gutted fishhooks. Such a holder, when plugged at the ends with corks, is waterproof, will not sink if dropped into the water, and is transparent so that you can see the hooks.

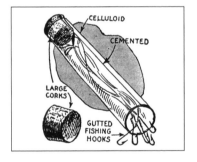

— FIRM ANGLEWORMS ASSURE A BIG STRING OF FISH —

When using angleworms for fish bait, anglers will find that trout and bass are more apt to strike them if they are kept fresh and firm. This is best done by lining the bottom of your bait box with swamp moss, which can be found in marshy woodlands. If the moss is not available in the woods, it can be obtained at your nearest florist. After covering the bottom of the bait box with moss, dampen it, place the day's supply of worms inside and cover them with more moss. The worms will be firm and fresh when the stream or lake is reached and they will remain in good condition for a full day's fishing.

— FLOATING BAIT BOX —

Fishermen will find the floating box shown in the drawing of considerable convenience because it is always within easy reach and, because it is submerged, it keeps the minnows alive. It is made from a piece of ¼-in. wire mesh about 18 in. long and 6 in. wide, the ends being soldered together to form a 6-in. cylinder. Two 6-in. tin-can covers are soldered on the ends. But before doing this the top cover is screwed to a wooden disk, cut from 1-in. material, and a 4-in. circular hole is cut through it and the tin cover, to permit getting the bait in and out. The box is tied to the boat by a cord attached to a staple in the cover.

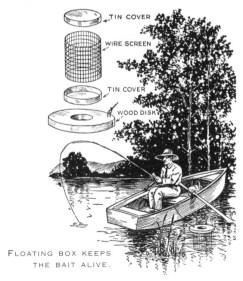

TIN COVER

WIRE SCREEN

TIN COVER

WOOD DISK

FLOATING BOX KEEPS THE BAIT ALIVE.

— MAKING FISHHOOKS EASILY DETACHABLE —

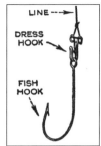

When one desires to remove a fishhook quickly from a line in order to substitute one of another style the knot is often too stiff to untie. An excellent and simple attachment that allows hooks to be removed and replaced easily is a common dress hook of large size, preferably one with a "hump," which locks the eye in place. The fish line is run through the eyes and tied, and the hook is slipped on as shown in the illustration. Dipping the hooks in black enamel or paint before using will render them less liable to be seen by the fish.

— MINNOW TROW —

Sheet metal and wire mesh are soldered together to form this handy little minnow trow, which will keep the fisherman's bait alive on the hottest day, when the usual minnow bucket, kept in the boat, would fail. In use, it is towed behind or alongside the boat and causes very little resistance because of its shape,

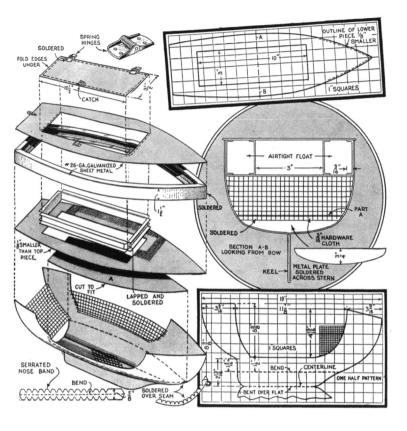

and thus it does not make rowing inconvenient due to drag. The wire-mesh sides permit a constant change of fresh, cool lake or river water, which is the reason for its success. Although the details given here were taken from a model that proved entirely satisfactory in actual use, you can make a larger one of similar proportions if desired. Airtight chambers keep it afloat even in rough weather, and as sheet metal is used for construction, the trow should last indefinitely.

𝒯𝒽ℯ PERFECT FLY

— QUICK-ACTING FLY VISE
HOLDS SPOOL AND THREAD —

This inexpensive fly vise consists of a dime-store metal clamp mounted on a slanting arm, which is in turn screwed to a wood base. The jaws are rounded at the ends with a file and are drilled partly through from the inside surfaces to take a spring, which spreads them as the tightening screws are loosened. When purchased, the rear screw does not pass entirely through both jaws. This screw hole is drilled out so that both screws can be driven in from the same side. Also, two small holes must be drilled in one jaw to mount the clamp on the supporting arm. A wooden peg set in the base holds the thread spool, and a tightly coiled spring mounted between two wooden brackets on the base serves as a holder for the loose end of the thread.

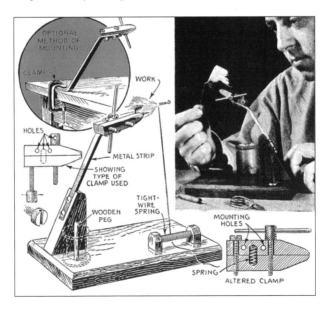

— DRYING FLIES —

The problem of drying flies is solved by one fisherman who puts them into a bottle of alcohol, inserts the cork and shakes the bottle. The alcohol absorbs the water quickly and evaporates almost instantly when the hook is exposed to air.

— EMERGENCY VISE FOR TYING FLIES —

When you are fishing and have to repair a fly, your pocketknife will make a good improvised vise for the purpose. Just stick the large blade into a log, bend the handle so that the point of the hook may be inserted in the hinge and allow it to close gently. The hook will be held securely and will not be injured.

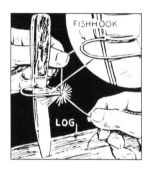

— FLY TYING —

Fly tying is one of the most interesting and useful of all the handicrafts. It can be fun to do and it serves a practical purpose. The basic principle of fly tying is the decoration of a fishhook so that it will attract fish. There are two types of flies that can be used under different circumstances: wet and dry. The dry fly sets on top of the water while the wet fly usually rests under the surface. Flies can be designed to simulate actual insects or improvised to

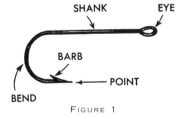

FIGURE 1

be completely artificial. To begin you must first know the different parts of the hook that you will use, *Figure 1*. The hook is the primary basis of the fly.

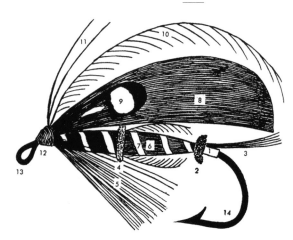

1. TAG
2. BUTT
3. TAIL
4. JOINT
5. HACKLE
6. BODY
7. RIBBING
8. WING
9. CHEEK
10. TOPPING
11. HORNS
12. HEAD
13. EYE
14. HOOK

FIGURE 2

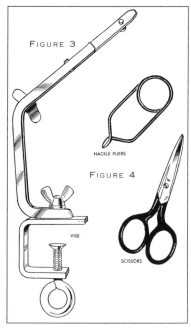

FIGURE 3

HACKLE PLIERS

FIGURE 4

VISE

SCISSORS

The next thing to study is the different parts of the fly, *Figure 2*. You will need a few tools. Some of these can be made, but they can all be bought at a small cost. The first item you will need is a vise, *Figure 3*. This is a cam-lever type, adjustable to various angles and hook sizes. The next item you will need is called hackle pliers, *Figure 4*. You will also need a pair of scissors with very sharp points. The materials used for fly tying are varied and they cover a wide range. You will need a piece of wax, a spool of tying silk, a bottle of lacquer, and some silk floss. To make the body of the fly you will also require some wool yarn and chenille, a few sizes of tinsel for ribbing, and assortment of neck and saddle hackles and some bucktails in three or four colors.

There are a number of other materials that can be added later when you have mastered the fundamentals of fly tying.

— BUCKTAIL STREAMERS —

Now you can begin by placing a hook in the vise and start waxed tying silk, *Figure 5*, ⅛ of an

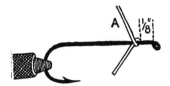

FIGURE 5

inch from the eye of the hook. Take five or six turns and cut off the end, *Figure 6*. Next wind the tying closely

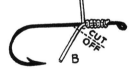

FIGURE 6

and evenly down the shank of the hook, *Figure 7*. Be sure you understand each step as you go along and work slowly at the beginning. The next step is important and a little more difficult: putting on the wings. Hold the tail material between your

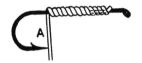

FIGURE 7

thumb and forefinger of the left hand. Slide the fingers down and over the hook so that the tail material rests on top of the hook, with the

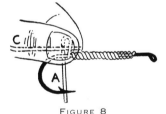

FIGURE 8

hook held firmly between your thumb and finger, *Figure 8*. Next loosen your grip a little to allow enough tying silk to pass between the thumb and tail material and down between the finger and material on the other side. Tighten your grip with thumb and finger and pull the loop down tight, and repeat once more, *Figure 9*.

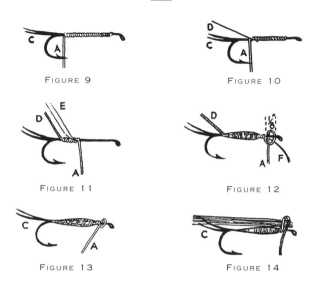

FIGURE 9

FIGURE 10

FIGURE 11

FIGURE 12

FIGURE 13

FIGURE 14

Now tie the tail in place with two turns of the tying silk (*A*) and tie in ribbing (*D*), *Figure 10.* Now take six or eight close tight turns with the tying silk toward the eye of the hook, and with two more turns tie in body material (*E*), *Figure 11.* If you are using body tinsel, be sure to cut the end to a taper before tying in as (*E*) *Figure 11.* This tends to make a smoother body and prevents a bunch where the material is tied in. Next wind tying silk (*A*) back to the starting point, take a half hitch and let it hang. Now wind body material (*E*) clockwise tightly and evenly back toward the bar, to the extreme rear

end of the body; pull tight and wind forward to within ⅛ of an inch of the eye, and wind back and forth to form a smooth tapered body, *Figure 12.* If you are using silk floss, untwist the floss and use only one-half or one-third strands. Do not let it twist, wind tightly, and it will make a nice smooth body. Take two turns and a half hitch with the tying silk and cut off the end of the material (*F*) *Figure 12.* Take one tight turn with ribbing (*D*) over the butt of tail close to rear end of the body, and also one turn under the tail if the tail is to be cocked. Wind the ribbing in a spiral around the body and tie it off with two turns and a half

FIGURE 15

FIGURE 16

hitch of tying silk, *Figure 13.* Take about three dozen hairs of colored bucktail. Cut off the butt ends to the length wanted for the finished fly, not more than one half again as long as the hook, place these on top of the hook, *Figure 14,* with the butt ends about 5/16th of an inch in back of the eye. Pull down two or three loops, *Figure 15.* Now take about 175 hairs of other colored bucktail, and place them on top of the first colored bucktail the same as *Figure 14.* Repeat the same operation as in *Figure 15.* Before finishing the head, put a drop of head lacquer on the butt of the hairs to cement them in place. Finish up by making a smooth tapered head with the tying silk (*Figure 16*). Take three or four half hitches, paint the head with two or three coats of lacquer, and your fly is ready to use.

— DRY FLIES —

This is one of the best all-purpose flies. Begin by winding the tying silk ⅛ of an inch from the eye of the hook. Be sure your silk is waxed. Take two or three turns toward the bend of the hook and cut off the end, *Figure 17.* Next cut a section about ¼ of an inch from a right and left wing feather, *Figure 18.* If you can, use duck wings because these are best for dry flies.

FIGURE 17

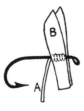

FIGURE 18

FIGURE 19

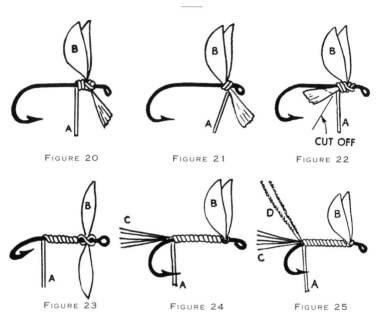

FIGURE 20   FIGURE 21   FIGURE 22

CUT OFF

FIGURE 23   FIGURE 24   FIGURE 25

Now place the convex sides together. Do not cut off the butt ends, but straddle the hook, *Figure 19.* Tip the wings forward, perpendicular to the shank, and pull down the loop, *Figure 20.* Take one more turn with the silk and before loosening the grip with the left hand, and take two turns around the hook close behind the wings, *Figure 21.* Now pull the butt ends back tightly as in *Figure 22,* take two tight turns around them, and cut off on the dotted line, *Figure 22.* Cross between the wings to spread them, and wind the tying silk down the shank of the hook, *Figure 23.*

From now on the body is made as previously explained, so for the sake of variation we will tie a band in the center the same as a Royal Coachman. Tie in the tail, *Figure 24.* Tie in two or three strands of peacock herl, *Figure 25,* and wind four or five turns toward the eye of the hook. Take three or four strands of silk floss, *Figure 26,* and take a few more turns over the loose ends toward the eye of the hook. Wind silk floss over the herl about halfway up the hook.

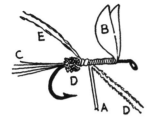

FIGURE 26

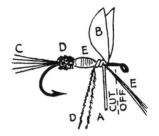

FIGURE 27

Take a turn or two around the silk floss and cut off the end, *Figure 27.* Carry it up to the front of the wings. (This helps to push the wings forward and to hold them in place.) Tie off the herl, *Figure 28.*

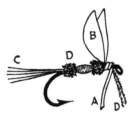

FIGURE 28

The next step of putting on the hackle is done as shown in *Figure 22.* The hackle is now much more important than on the wet fly. The floating qualities of the dry fly depend almost entirely upon a stiff neck hackle of the right size. Often two hackles are used, laid together, with both butts tied in at the same time. One hackle of the proper size and stiffness is usually enough, so we will use one tied as in *Figure 19,* and explained in *Figure 22.* Clip the hackle pliers to the tip of hackle and wind about two turns edgewise in front of the wings. Then wind two turns close in back of the wings.

Take two or three more turns in front of the wings, keeping the hackle edgewise, with the shiny side toward the eye of the hook. Wind the hackle close so as not to fill up the eye of the hook, and so as to leave room for the head. Tie in the tip with a couple of turns, *Figure 29.* The hackle should now be standing straight out from the hook, with most of it in front of the wings. Now shape a tapered head. The head should be about 1/16 inch long on a size 12 hook, *Figure 30.* Finish with two or three half hitches and a drop of head lacquer, *Figure 31.*

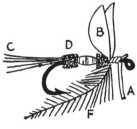

FIGURE 29

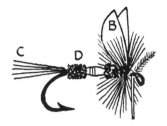

FIGURE 30

Various types of feathers are used for wings of dry flies. The best are breast feathers from mallard, teal partridge, grouse, black duck, or wood duck. Hackle tips are best with feathers from starling, duck, turkey, goose pheasant, wing feathers, etc.

Two whole feathers of the proper size with the natural curve are used for fan wings. The tips of two feathers, or a section, may be cut from two

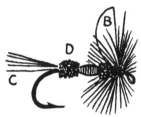

FIGURE 31

matched feathers. All of these wings are tied on in the same manner as previously explained.

— FLOATING BUGS —

Some of the greatest attractions for fish are floating bugs. These can be made of a variety of materials. Let us begin by making a simple one. If you follow the instructions carefully and look at the illustrations, you will be rewarded in your first effort by an effective floating bug. As in other procedures,

remember to wax your silk thoroughly. Take a few turns around the shank of the hook and tie in a small bunch of hairs for the tail, *Figure 32*. Now clip a small bunch of hairs about the size of a match, close to the hide. If there is some fuzz mixed with the hair at the base close to the skin, pick out the fuzz and place the

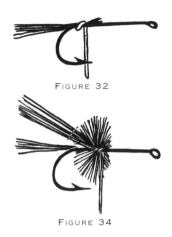

FIGURE 32

FIGURE 34

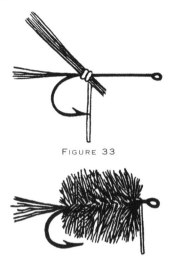

FIGURE 33

FIGURE 35

butts of the hairs under the hook, *Figure 33*.

Now take a couple of turns with the tying silk, hold the tips of the hair with the thumb and forefinger of the left hand, and pull the tying silk tight. Notice that the hairs spin around the hook and the butt ends stand out at right angles to the hook, *Figure 34*.

Now cut off the tip ends of the hairs and then press them back tightly. Apply a drop of lacquer to the base of the hairs and the hook, and repeat the same process of tying on a small bunch of hair each time, pressing it back slightly. Remember that the hair must be close together to make a smooth, even body. Your body should now be built up so that it looks like *Figure 35*.

At this stage remove it from your vise and with your scissors, and trim it so it looks like *Figures 36* and *37*. Now you should have about ³/₁₆th of an inch of the shank of the hook left just behind the eye. This is where you will tie on your wings. Cover this bare hook with well waxed tying silk, and lay a bunch of hair on top of the hook for wings, *Figure 38*.

Crisscross the silk around the wings and the hook until they are firmly tied. Put on several coats of lacquer over the juncture of the wings and the hook so that they will remain secure. After you have lacquered the wings, let them dry. Then

FIGURE 36

FIGURE 39

FIGURE 37

press them flat and trim them as shown in *Figure 39.*

You now have a completed bug. You can create your own designs using any color you want to suit your own fancy.

FIGURE 38

CLEANING *the* CATCH

— RATTRAP FOR SCALING FISH —

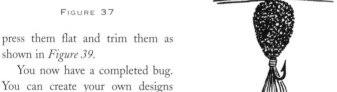

A novel and convenient device for cleaning and scaling fish is shown in the accompanying illustration. It consists of a rattrap with the bait pan removed and several steel nails driven into the wooden base near the edge. The points are left projecting about ½ in. and are filed sharp. The trap is fastened to a post at a convenient height, and in use, the trap jaw is raised and the tail of the fish placed upon the projecting brads. Releasing the jaw presses the brads into the tail so that the fish will hang head downward at a convenient height for scaling.

— SKIN PULLED OFF CATFISH EASILY WITH A PAIR OF PLIERS —

You can skin a catfish easily with a pair of pliers. First kill it with a sharp blow on the head. Then cut off the fins and drive a nail through the head and into a board. With a sharp knife, cut through the skin around the fish just back of the head. Now grasp the edge of the skin with a pair of pliers and pull back toward the tail.

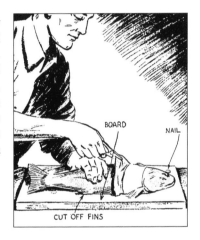

— ❖ ❖ ❖ —

THE BOATING LIFE

WHAT'S CANOE?

— HOW TO BUILD A CANOE —

Canoe-making is commonly considered more difficult than building the larger and heavier craft, but many amateurs with only ordinary experience and tools have turned out satisfactory canoes. If the simple directions given here are carefully followed, the work will proceed rapidly and no difficulty will be encountered. Working with light materials, the canoe builder must pay particular attention to the workmanship. Because it is many times more difficult to patch up mistakes in a canoe than it is in rowboats or other heavier craft, the work must not be hurried; plenty of time should be taken to do each and every part well and in a workmanlike manner.

The craft described—the regulation "open" or Canadian model— is comparatively light and draws very little water. It is not a flimsy makeshift but a stiff and thoroughly dependable canoe designed for long service. Barring accidents and given reasonably good care, the canoe will continue to give satisfaction for many years.

The tools needed are the common

ones found in most homes, consisting of rip and crosscut saws, chisel, screwdriver, drawknife, awl, brace and bits, rule hammer, vise, plane, and three or four cheap wood, or metal, screw clamps. The list of materials given is for a canoe about 16 ft. long, with a 31-in. beam, an 18-in. depth at the ends, 12½-in. depth amidships, and weighing from 60 to 70 pounds depending on the material used.

Although oak or ash makes the best stems, other woods may be used; rock elm and fir are very satisfactory substitutes. Where cedar is specified, spruce pine, cypress, or fir may likewise be employed. The materials for molds and ribbands, which are required to give form to the craft, may be cut from any cheap stuff, and this will reduce the cost somewhat.

Materials

STEM: 1 piece oak or ash, 6 ft. long and ¾ in. square.

KEELSON (inside keel): 1 piece oak or ash, 14 ft. long, 3½ in. wide, ⅜ in. thick.

GUNWALES: 2 pieces oak or ash, 16 ft. long, ⅞ in. wide, ½ in. thick.

SEAT RISINGS: 2 pieces oak or ash, ½ in. square.

FENDERWALES: 34 ft. ½-in., half-round molding. Oak or ash best for hard knocks.

OUTSIDE KEEL: (may be omitted if desired): 1 piece oak, 14 ft. by 1 in., ½ in. thick.

DECK BEAMS: 2 pieces oak or ash, 8 in. long, 1⅛ in. wide, ⅜ in. thick.

SEAT FRAMES: 2 pieces oak or ash, 30 in. long, 3 in. wide, ¾ in. thick.

SEAT FRAMES: 2 pieces oak or ash, 12 in. long, 2¼ in. wide, ¾ in. thick.

PLANKING: cedar or pine, 100 sq. ft., ⅛ in. thick. Best secured by purchasing 25 ft. of 1-in. lumber, and having same dressed on two sides to ⅛ in. thick, and in lengths of 12, 14, and 16 ft. This will give the minimum amount of waste.

BACKBONE: 1 piece cedar or pine, any cheap stuff, 16 ft. long, 4 in. wide, ⅞ in. thick.

MOLDS: 1 piece any cheap stuff, 16 ft. long, 1 ft. wide, ⅞ in. thick.

RIBBANDS: 8 pieces any cheap stuff, 14 ft. long, ¾ in. wide, ½ in. thick.

RIBS: 360 running feet, cedar, 1¾ in. wide, ⅛ in. thick.

BREAST HOOKS FOR DECKS:
1 piece cedar or oak, 32 in. long, 9 in. wide, ¾ in. thick.
1 lb. 2-in. wire nails to make form for keel.
1 lb. ⅝-in. copper clout nails, for fastening ribs.
½ lb. ¾-in. copper clout nails, for fastening seat risings.
18 1¼-in. No. 8 brass screws, for fastening decks and deck beams.

24 1-in. No. 6 brass screws, for fastening seats.
4 lb. patent marine glue to cement canvas to planking.
3 oz. No. 2 copper tacks to fasten canvas with.
11¾ yd. No. 6 ounce canvas for covering hull.
1 lb. ⅜-in. copper tacks to fasten planking to ribs.

— BACKBONE AND MOLDS —

The first step in the construction of a canoe is to get out the backbone and the molds—or forms—that give the correct dimensions and shape of the craft. The backbone may be made from any inexpensive softwood, such as cedar, spruce, pine, or cypress; for making it, a piece of lumber, 16 ft. long, 4 in. wide, and ⅞ in. thick, is used. By referring to Figure 1 it will be seen that the upper edge measures exactly 15 ft. 8¾ in., and that the lower edge is ½ in. longer, giving a total length of 15 ft. 9¼ in. The spaces numbered from each end of the backbone toward the center, as 1, 2, 3, and 4, indicate where the corresponding molds are to be placed. Seven molds are used and because a canoe is tapered alike at both ends, the molds are numbered alike and are made to exactly the same dimensions.

A good way to lay out the

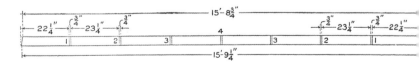

FIGURE 1. THE FIRST STEP IN THE CONSTRUCTION OF A CANOE IS TO GET OUT THE BACKBONE AND THE MOLDS, OR FORMS, WHICH GIVE THE CORRECT DIMENSIONS AND SHAPE OF THE CRAFT.

backbone accurately is to first mark the total length, making the lower edge 1 in. longer than represented in *Figure 1*. Then measure along the top edge exactly 22¼ in. and run a pencil line across. From this line measure off ¾ in. and draw a second line across the width of the board parallel with the first. This space represents the thickness of the mold, and it is

marked 1. Measure off 23¼ in. and make two parallel lines as before and number it 2; measure another 23¼-in. length and number it 3. Begin measuring from the opposite end of the board as in the first instance, 22¼ in. and give it number 1, then mark off 2 and 3 the same as for the end already marked. The board is then cut off at the bevel mark at each end.

— Molds or Forms —

The molds that give form to the hull are shown and numbered in the order that they are fastened to the backbone. To get out No. 1 mold draw a rectangle on a sheet of stiff paper exactly 13⅜ in. long and 11 in. wide as shown in *Figure 2*. Run cross lines to divide it in quarters and mark out the center mortise for the backbone, which is 5 in. deep and ⅞ in. wide. Measure 4 in. toward each side from the outside edge of the backbone mortise and mark the mortises for receiving the gunwales, which are

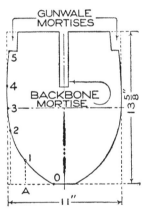

FIGURE 2.

1⅝ in. long and ¾ in. wide or deep.

To obtain the correct bilge curve lay the rule on the bottom line and measure off exactly 1 in. to the left of the center dividing line and make dot 0. Measure 2¾ in. farther to the left, to *A*; turn the rule at right angles and measure 2⅛ in. inside the line and make dot 1. Measure 1½ in. to the left of *A*, turn rule at right angles and measure up the sheet exactly 4⅞ in. and make dot 2, which will be ¼ in. inside of the left vertical line. On the center horizontal line, which

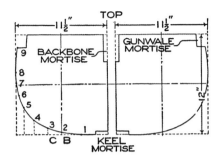

TOP

BACKBONE MORTISE

GUNWALE MORTISE

9
8
7
6
5
4
3 2 1

C B KEEL MORTISE

.FIGURE 3. IT IS MORE CONVENIENT TO MAKE EACH MOLD IN TWO SECTIONS, BECAUSE TWO COMPLETE MOLDS ARE REQUIRED.

is 1¹⁵/₁₆ in. above dot 2, mark dot 3, ¹/₁₆ in. from the left vertical line. Measure off 2 in. above the horizontal center line and make dot 4 on the vertical line. The space between these two dots is the widest part of the bilge curve. Lay the rule on the bottom line of the gunwale mortise and measure off ³/₁₆ in. from the outside line and make dot 5. Pencil the angle from dot to dot and draw in the full curve. Cut out the half section, fold on the vertical center line, and draw the right side.

Two complete No. 2 molds are required, but it is more convenient to make each mold in two sections. Each half is made 11½ in. wide and 12 in. deep, as shown in *Figure 3*. First draw a rectangle to these

dimensions and run cross lines to divide it into quarters. Beginning at the upper right-hand corner, mark the mortises for gunwales and backbone, which, being only one-half of the complete form, will be ⁷/₁₆ in. wide and 3¼ in. deep.

Laying the rule on the outside line immediately below the mortise, draw a second mortise for the keel, which is ⅜ in. deep and 1½ in. wide in the half section. Measure off 1¾ in. to the left along the bottom line from the keel mortise and make dot 1. Dot 2 is made by measuring 2½ in. to the left of 1, turning the rule at right angles at *B* and measuring ⁵/₁₆ in. inside the line as shown in the sketch. Make dot 3 at a point 1¾ in. to the left of 2 and ¾ in. inside of the line. Dot 4 is 1¾ in. from *C* and 1¾ in. inside of the line. Dot 5 is 1¼ in. farther to the left and 3¼ in. inside of the line. Dot 6 is ⅝ in. from dot 5 and 4 ¾ in. inside of the line, which will bring it ³/₈ in. inside of the left vertical line. At a point 1½ in. above 6 make dot 7 above it. Between the dots 7 and 8 is the widest part of the bilge curve. Dot 9 is exactly ¼ in. inside of the vertical marginal line. These dots produce the angles, and it is only necessary to trace in the full curve and cut it out to make a pattern for the other three half sections needed.

The two No. 3 molds, *Figure 4,* are located near the center of the canoe and are made a trifle wider. Make a rectangle 14⅜ in. long by 12 in. wide and draw a cross line dividing it into quarters. Trace the half mortises for the backbone, gunwale, and keel from the No. 2 mold pattern. Lay the rule on the bottom line and measure off ½ in. to the left from the center vertical line and mark dot 1, which is the beginning of the bilge curve. At a point 2¾ in. to the left and ¾ in. inside of the line place dot 2, and 2 in. to the left of this and 2¼ in. inside of the line

place dot 3, then 1⅛ in. farther to the left, turn the rule at right angles and measure up 4 in. inside of the line for dot 4, which is ¹³/₁₆ in. inside of the left marginal line. At a point 2 in. above dot 4 make dot 5 on the marginal line and 2⅛ in. above it make dot 6. The space between gives the widest part of the bilge curve, with dot 7 exactly ¼ in. inside of the marginal line, measuring along the bottom of the gunwale mortise. Trace the angle and from it run the full curve and use this for a pattern for cutting out the other molds.

Mold No. 4 is placed amidships in the center of the canoe and only one complete mold is required, as shown in *Figure 5.* To make a pattern draw a rectangle 15 in. long and 12 in. wide, and divide it into four equal parts as before. From the No. 3 mold pattern trace in the mortises for the gunwale, backbone, and keel. Lay the rule on the bottom outside line and measure 2 in. from the centerline to the left at *D* and turn the rule at right angles and measure off ⁵/₁₆ in.

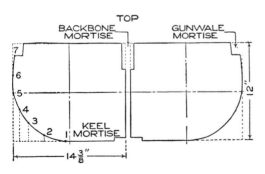

FIGURE 4. THIS MOLD IS LOCATED NEAR THE CENTER OF A CANOE AND IS MADE A TRIFLE WIDER.

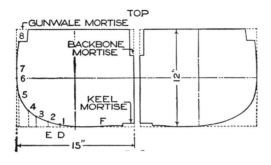

FIGURE 5. THIS MOLD IS PLACED AMIDSHIPS, IN THE CENTER OF THE CANOE, AND ONLY ONE IS REQUIRED.

widest part of the correct bilge curve. Exactly 3¾ in. above dot 7 and ¼ in. inside of the vertical side line make dot 8, which marks the beginning of the bilge curve above the water line and at the gunwale mortise.

The curve of the canoe floor is quite flat, but not exactly a straight line. Lay the rule on the bottom line and measure up, on the inner edge of the keel mortise, ⅛ in. Then 2½ in. to the left make a mark, F, 1/16 in. inside the bottom line. A pencil line drawn between them will enable one to trace the correct curve. Having cut out the pattern, make two wood forms exactly alike to have it complete, as shown. After finishing the seven complete molds, fasten them securely together by nailing a couple of battens across the halves.

inside of the bottom line and make dot 1. Measure, from D, 1½ in. to E, turn the rule up and measure off ⅝ in. inside the line and make dot 2. Dot 3 is 1½ in. farther to the left and 1¼ in. inside the line and dot 4 is 1 in. to the left of 3 and 2 in. inside of the line. Dot 5 is 1¼ in. to the left of dot 4, and 4 in. inside of the bottom line, which will bring it ¼ in. inside of the left vertical sideline. At a point 2 in. above dot 5 make dot 6 on the outside vertical line and 1¼ in. above it make dot 7. The space between dots 6 and 7 gives the

— RIBBANDS AND STEMS —

The ribbands are merely strips of wood, ¾ in. wide, ½ in. thick, and 14 ft. long. Any cheap stuff will do because they are only used to give the correct shape of the canoe curve while building it. Six ribbands are necessary, and it is best to use eight lengths in order to make sure that the ribs are bent at the required angle and that both sides of the canoe are ribbed at the one uniform curve. For the stems, use ash or oak, ¾ in. square, and straight-grained material must be selected because it is necessary to bend it to obtain the requisite curve.

To make the pattern for the stem mold shown in *Figure 6*, draw a rectangle 24½ in. long by 12 in. wide, and divide it into four equal parts. Lay the rule on the left side at the upper corner, at *G*, measure down 1 in. and make dot 1. Lay the rule along the top horizontal line and measure 2½ in. from *G* and make dot 2, then draw a pencil line between them. From dot 1 measure along this line exactly ¾ in. and make dot 3. From dot 2 measure straight down 1¾ in. to *H*, turn at right angles and measure off ⅝ in. to the right and make dot 4. Make a pencil line from 2 to 4 as shown.

From dot 2 lay the rule parallel with the top horizontal line and measure off 9¾ in., turn at right angles and measure down on the center line 2¼ in. and make dot 5.

Lay the rule at the upper right corner and measure down the vertical line 2¾ in., turn the rule at right angles and measure off 3⅞ in. and make dot 6. From the upper right-hand corner measure off 1⅝ in. and make dot 7 exactly ¼ in. inside the top horizontal line. Again place the rule at the right-hand corner, measure down the vertical line exactly 2 in. and make dot 8. Draw the line from dot 7 to 8, and ½ in. from dot 8, make dot 9. This gives the correct contour of the stem where it joins the splice of the keel.

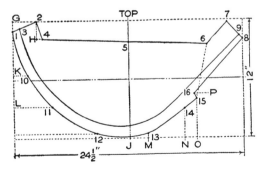

FIGURE 6. STRAIGHT-GRAINED MATERIAL MUST BE SELECTED FOR THE STEMS, BECAUSE IT IS NECESSARY TO BEND THEM TO SHAPE.

The greatest curve and width of the stem is at *J* on the lower line. To obtain the correct curve begin at the upper left corner and measure from dot 1 down the vertical line 4½ in. to *K.* Turn the rule at right angles and measure 1¼ in. inside the line, and make dot 10. Dot 11 is placed by measuring down from *K* exactly 3¼ in. to *L,* when the rule is turned at right angles and a length of 4 in. measured off inside of the line. Dot 12 is located in the same manner by measuring 2¾ in. below *L* and running 8¾ in. inside the line, as shown.

To finish the irregular curve of the stem, measure from *J* at the center of the lower horizontal line 2 in. to *M,* turn the rule up and measure off ½ in. inside of the line, and make

dot 13. Dot 14 is made by measuring off 4 in. from *M* to *N* and turning the rule to a point 3 in. inside the line, as shown. Then from point *N* measure to *O* 1¼ in., and then measure up 4 in. to dot 15. From the dot 14 to 15 run a straight line. The dot 15 should be exactly 5 in. inside of the right vertical line.

Allowance for the beveled splice of the stem to the inside keel must now be made, and the beginning is to run a light pencil line from dot 15 to dot 6. From dot 15 measure up ½ in., turn the rule at *P* and make dot 16 exactly ¼ in. to the left of the upright line. From dot 16 a line is run to dot 8, which completes the angle of the curve. The full curve is then easily traced in.

— INSIDE KEEL, OR KEELSON —

The inside keel—or keelson— is made exactly 13 ft. 11 in. long and 3½ in. wide in the center,

which is, of course, amidships. It is unnecessary to go to the trouble of making a paper pattern for this

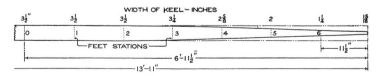

because the keel is merely tapered uniformly from center to ends, and this may be drawn on the surface of the board directly. The board being 13 ft. 11 in. long and 3½ in. wide, it is only necessary to make cross lines exactly in the center both ways. From the center measure 1 ft. toward one end and make the width at that point 3½ in. Measure 1 ft. farther along, and again make the width 3½ in. as before. Continue in this manner, making the third station 3¼ in.; the fourth, 2⅝ in.; the fifth, 2 in.; the sixth, 1¼ in.; and the width at the ends 15/16 in. This detail is shown in *Figure 7*. Bend the stem on the mold and fasten it to the keel by means of a couple of ¾-in. No. 10 screws at each end.

— RIBS AND GUNWALES —

The ribs are best made of cedar, cut from the same material as the planking. They are 1¾ in. wide and ⅛ in. thick. It is a good plan to saw out several long lengths and cut them off as required, the length being determined by measuring from gunwale to gunwale around the curve over the ribbands. The ribs are put in under the ribbands, and the thickness of the latter will allow sufficient wood for making a good fit at the sheer line. The gunwales are two straight strips, 16 ft. long, ⅞ in. wide, and ½ in. thick.

— SETTING UP THE CANOE —

Having made all the material ready, the work of setting up the canoe may begin. As it is built upside down, place the backbone on boxes about 1 ft. or more above the floor, and place the molds in the numbered places on the backbone, allowing the backbone to rest upon the bottom of the mortises cut in the top of the molds. Study *Figures 8* and *9* before beginning the work of setting up the hull.

True up the molds with a square and fasten them firmly by toenailing them to the backbone. Put the keelson in place, allowing it to fit down in the mortises cut in the molds to receive it. Take particular care that the stems are a good fit with the angle of the backbone at the ends,

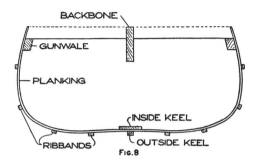

FIGURE 8. THE RIBS ARE FASTENED TO THE OUTSIDE OF THE KEELSON AND ARE CURVED UNDER THE RIBBANDS.

and then fasten by nailing through the top edge of the mold into the stems. As shown in the stem mold drawing, *Figure 6*, the splice where the stem fits the keelson must be cut out after it is bent into place. This is easily done by marking around the outside edge of the stem and then beveling from the inside on each side. The outer edge is left about ⅛ in. wide, and the bevel runs out to the width of the keel at the lower end.

The gunwales are next put on at the sheer line and fastened to the molds and stems, leaving sufficient of the nails exposed to make them easily withdrawn later on. The four ribbands are then put on each side at equal distances apart, between the gunwale and keel, or at 5-in. centers, measuring from the keel up toward the gunwale. Fasten the ribbands by

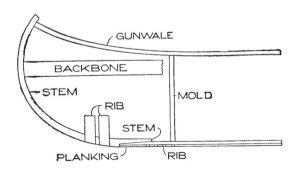

FIGURE 9. THE BENT STEM IS FASTENED TO THE KEEL WITH SCREWS AT BOTH ENDS.

driving the 1¼-in. brads through them into the mold. Measure off the keel for the ribs, which should be put on 3 in. apart, measuring from the centers. The ribs are fastened to the outside of the keelson and are curved under the ribbands. Fasten each rib to the keel by means of two ⅝-in. copper clout nails, then spring them into place and fasten to the gunwales. Put all the ribs in the same way, spacing them so that a rib will be placed over each mold. When all the ribs are put in, remove the ribbands and begin planking the hull.

— PLANKING THE CANOE —

Because a canoe is planked with ⅛-in. cedar it is easily bent to the curve of the ribs while cold, thus doing away with the trouble of steaming. Unlike heavier-planked craft, the planking of this canoe is not rabbeted at the stem but is nailed to the beveled surface. For strength, and to give a perfectly smooth skin on which to lay the canvas, it is advisable to run the planking the full length from stem to stem.

Begin by putting on the garboard strake, which is the bottom plank at the keel. Punch holes in the plank with an awl, not directly in line but staggered from side to side along the ribs. This will prevent the possibility of splitting. Drive in the copper clout nails while the plank is kept in place with a clamp to facilitate the work. Hold a clinch iron, or any handy piece of iron, inside and clinch the nails so that the ends are well embedded in the rib on the inside. It is a simple matter to fit each plank in place, because they are merely a close fit at the edge, butted together without beveling.

The number of planks required will depend upon the width, and while wider strips may be used, planking cut to the width of 3 in. is generally employed. In any case the top plank or sheer strake should be level with the gunwale from one stem to the other. When the hull is completely planked, cut off the ends of the planking to the curve of the stems and gunwales. The backbone and molds may now be taken out by sawing the backbone in two. Tack a couple of strips across the gunwales to keep the hull from sagging out of shape, then drive the nails over the sections the molds occupied, since these forms prevented doing this work before.

— SEAT RISINGS AND SEATS —

The seat risings are simply straight sticks, ½ in. square, and are fastened on the inside for the seats to rest upon. They are about 4 in. below the gunwale. Oak or ash is the best material, and the length

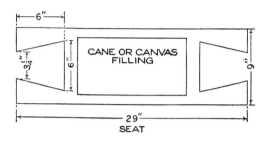

FIGURE 10. THE SEAT FRAME MAY BE CANED, OR A CANVAS SEAT TACKED ON, AS PREFERRED.

is 14 ft. To fasten in place, first bore a small hole and then nail through the planking and ribs and clinch on the inside of the rising.

The seat frame is fashioned as shown in *Figure 10,* and may be caned or a canvas seat tacked on, as preferred. Many canoeists prefer to kneel, in which case a seat bar, about 4 or 5 in. wide, is run across for the paddler's back and thighs to rest against while paddling.

— DECK BEAMS AND DECKS —

The deck beams are merely straight pieces, about 8 in. long, 1⅛ in. wide, and ⅜ in. thick. These are notched at the ends as shown in *Figure 11,* so that they will come up and wedge against the sides of the gunwales about ½ in. Put them in by boring a hole through the gunwale and fasten with a 1¼-in. No. 10 screw at each end. Two are required, one at each end.

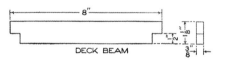

FIGURE 11.

The deck, or breast, hooks are made 16 in. long by 8 in. wide and of the shape shown in *Figure 12.* To fasten them in place bore three holes through the deck into the deck beam

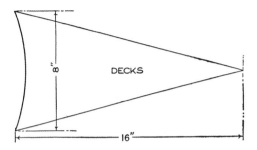

FIGURE 12. THE SHAPE OF THE DECK OR BREAST
HOOKS AND THE BEAMS THAT SUPPORT THEM.

and secure them with three 1¼-in. No. 10 screws. Bore three holes along the gunwale on each side and turn three 1¼-in. No. 10 screws into the deck.

— A Center Thwart —

To strengthen and stiffen the hull a center thwart, or cross bar, should be run across the canoe amidships. A piece of oak or ash, ⅜ in. thick and tapering from 2 in. in the center to 1 in. at the ends, should be screwed to the lower side of the gunwale. Although not exactly essential, it is a good plan to run another thwart across the canoe just back of the forward seat, and a rear thwart some 3 ft. forward of the rear seat, or paddling bar. This will make the craft very stiff when a heavy load is carried, and likewise prevent the lightly constructed hull from sagging, or "hogging," when stored for the winter.

— Applying the Canvas —

The canvas is put on with marine glue, the black kind being the best for this particular purpose. Before gluing the canvas, lay it smoothly on the hull and trim so that it will fold nicely at the stems, as shown in *Figure 13*. Melt the

FIGURE 13. THE MANNER OF SHAPING
THE ENDS OF THE CANVAS TO FIT
OVER THE CANOE ENDS.

glue in a can over a moderately hot fire and spread it on one side of the canvas with a stiff brush. Of course, the glue will be too thick to spread evenly, but be sure to apply it as evenly as possible, and touch every bit of the canvas with a fairly heavy coating of glue. Lay the glued canvas in place, and iron with a moderately hot flatiron. This melts the glue and allows the canvas to adhere smoothly to the planking. Finish by tacking the edge of the canvas along the edge off the gunwales, and fold the canvas as smoothly as possible at the stem. Tack it in place, running the line of tacks exactly down the centerline of the stem.

— Fenders or Covering Strips —

Fenders of ½-in. round molding may be tacked on to cover the edge of the canvas, or a 1 in. wide strip may be sawed from the same material as the planking and tacked to cover the edge by using 1¼-in. brads every 2 or 3 in. along the edge.

— Stem Bands and Outside Keel —

The stem bands may be made from wood if desired and bent to shape, but the brass oval stem or bang iron, ⅜ in. wide, makes a stronger and better finish. The wood stem band should be ⅜ in. square and rounded on the outside. Put this on with 1¼-in. brads and fasten the brass band with ¾-in. screws.

The outside keel may or may not be used, according to preference. It strengthens the canoe to a certain extent and keeps the bottom from many a scratch while pulling out. The usual outside keel is about 1 in. wide and ½ in. thick, of oak or ash, and tapered at the stems to the width of the stem bands, which are screwed on over it. The most serviceable keel is about 2½ in. wide in the center, and tapers to fit the bands at either end. When made of ⅜-in. oak or ash, it makes a splendid protection for the bottom of the hull, especially when the craft is used in rocky waters. Unlike the narrow keel, the flat keel makes the canoe easier to turn with the paddle. But any form of keel will add several pounds to the weight of the craft and for this reason is often omitted.

— Painting the Canoe —

The canvas should be given a coat of shellac before the paint is applied. This makes it waterproof. Then four coats of paint are applied to fill the fibers of the canvas. To make a smooth finishing coat, rub down the second and third coats with fine sandpaper. The entire woodwork of the canoe should be finished with three coats of good quality outside spar varnish.

A slatted grating, made of softpine lattice stuff, about 1⅛ in. wide and 1¼ in. thick, will afford protection to the bottom of the canoe. For summer use this is desirable, but may be omitted on long trips and when soft footwear is worn. The grating should not be fastened to the ribs, but the parallel strips screwed, or nailed, to cross strips, curved to fit the contour of the canoe's bottom. The grating should extend from well under the stern seat up to the stem splice in the bow, and should be nicely tapered to make a neat appearance. By fastening two or three little blocks of wood so that they will extend up between the slats, one may screw small brass buttons into these blocks to keep the slatted floor in place, thus making it easily removable when washing out the canoe.

— Ornamental Figureheads for Canoes —

If you want to be the first in your neighborhood to have something really attractive and novel in the boat line, make some figureheads for your canoe. Figureheads, you may know, were always attached to the prows of old ships as a sort of an emblem of good luck. They were carved in beautiful, grained woods, and some that have been preserved in the marine museums are works of art. So, just as a good-luck charm, let's see what can be done to decorate the bow of the canoe.

The illustration suggests four different models that can be used and, of course, your personal likes will suggest many more than can be as easily made. If you have no artistic ability, let an artist friend trace out the shape and suggest the coloring. The figure chosen for your

ORNAMENTAL FIGUREHEADS OF A GOOSE, A MOOSE, OR ANY OTHER
SUITABLE DESIGN, ARE DISTINCTIVE AND NOVEL, AND
THEY CAN READILY BE MADE BY ANYONE
HAVING SOME ARTISTIC ABILITY.

decorative scheme must be one that will lend itself to being shaped to fit the curved end of the canoe. Thus the goose, the moose, and the bear fit the purpose admirably.

The selected one can be marked out in pencil on the surface of a smooth piece of soft pine, cedar, cypress or any suitable wood, which is easily sawed and whittled. When the outline and details are drawn in,

saw out the portions that can be reached with a keyhole saw. Then cut out all smaller details of the edges with a sharp jackknife until the final outline is finished. After that, go over the edges and both sides with fine sandpaper. Draw in the details again with a soft pencil and give the board a coating of shellac. Prime the board with flat white paint and, when dry, the details can be painted in. As the outlines of the details will show faintly through the priming coat, no redrawing will be found necessary. Use artists' colors if possible and work from a colored print to get the coloring correct.

When completed on both sides, set aside to dry for several days. After the paint has hardened, the surface should be given an application of good spar or automobile varnish. Do not use floor varnish, because this will become white when wet.

Screw a thin strip of oak to the curved part of the back of the figure and let it project 2 or 3 in. at each end. Then, after removing the brass molding from part of the bow, screw the strip in its place. This will support the figurehead in front of and at the top of the bow as seen in the illustration.

— CANOE SEARCHLIGHT ROTATED BY TURNING A CRANK —

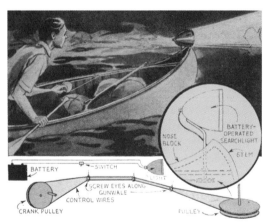

rotated by means of a crank located within easy reach from the paddling position. Any auto headlight or spotlight can be used for the purpose, and is attached to a vertical shaft that passes through a block fitted under the nose block. It is fitted with a collar attached with a setscrew to hold the shaft at the desired height. The lower detail shows the pulley-and-crank arrangement by which the searchlight is turned, the rope passing through

When canoeing at night, this searchlight enables you to observe the shoreline without turning the canoe as would be the case if the light were stationary, because it can be screw eyes driven into the gunwale. A small storage battery is fastened to the canoe with clamps, which prevent losing it in case the canoe is upset. A switch is located near the crank. The switch is cut in one of the lines leading from the battery to the light as can be seen in the circuit diagram.

— CANOE CARRIED SINGLE-HANDED —

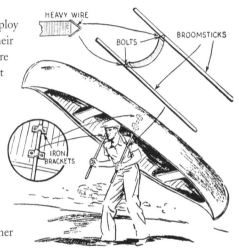

Sportsmen who employ a light canoe on their hunting or fishing trips are often obliged to carry it around rapids or shallows. If two pieces of broomstick are provided with a canvas shoulder strap, as shown, they may be used to carry the boat much more conveniently. The ends of the handles fit into iron brackets screwed to the inner surfaces of the canoe.

— DETACHABLE CANVAS SEAT IN A BOAT ACCOMMODATES EXTRA PERSON —

This boat seat, which is made from heavy canvas, comes in handy when carrying an extra passenger. It hooks into screw eyes driven into the boat sides and is quickly removed and rolled up when not in use.

PADDLE POWER

— BUILDING A SECTIONAL FLAT-BOTTOM ROWBOAT —

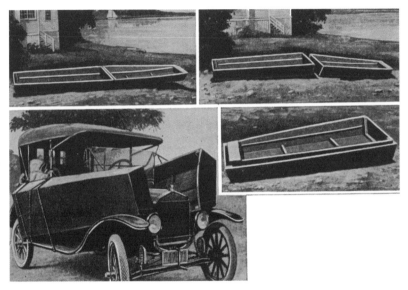

ABOVE: THE BOAT SECTIONS SHOWN FASTENED TOGETHER AND SEPARATE.
BELOW RIGHT: THE SECTIONS NESTED FOR TRANSPORTATION.
LEFT: THE BOAT LASHED TO THE RUNNING BOARD OF AN AUTOMOBILE.

A novel form of flat-bottom rowboat is shown in the illustrations; this boat has been found very handy on hunting and fishing trips. The boat is made in two sections and may be transported easily on a light auto. Another desirable feature is that, if two men have crossed a stream and one desires to return before the other, he can disconnect and use one section for his purpose, leaving the other section for his partner.

The materials necessary for the construction of the boat are: two boards, ⅝ by 12 in. by 16 ft., for the

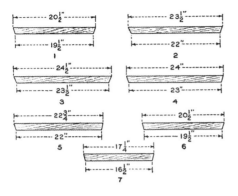

bottom; two pieces, ½ by 12 in. by 16 ft., for the sides; one board, 1 by 12 in. by 7 ft., for the ends and centers; two boards, ½ by 5 in. by 16 ft., for footboards, all of cypress; 30 ft. of screen-door molding, for seat rail; one piece, 1½ by 3 in. by 6 ft., for end braces and cleats; one piece, 1½ by 1½ in. by 15 ft., for cleats, to be of spruce, the lumber surfaced on all sides; one box of No. 8 flat-head screws, 1½ in. long; 2 lb. of shingle nails, and twelve 2½-in. stove bolts with washers.

Having obtained these materials, the construction is begun by cutting six cleats from the 1½ by 1½-in. stock. Both center cleats are the same length; the end cleats are cut from the 1½ by 3-in. material. Care must be taken that these pieces fit

exactly, otherwise the flare will not be correct, and the cleats will not fit the sides of the boat, when finished. Next, take the two boards that are to form the bottoms, lay them edge to edge, insert a 1-in. strip of tar paper that has been well coated with roofing cement in the joint, and clamp together. This forms the rough outline of the boat bottom. Then take the two center cleats and nail them in position loosely, with a tar paper gasket between the planks and cleats. The cleats are nailed so that their inner edges are 2¼ in. apart. When properly set, turn over the planks and screw the bottom to the cleats with four or more screws to each cleat. The remaining cleats and the end braces are applied in the same manner, in the positions shown in the drawing.

After all the cleats have been set, the planks must be trimmed off at the sides and ends, with a bevel equal to that of the cleat ends. Having done this, the bottom of the boat is finished. The next step is to cut the ends and centerboards as shown in the drawing, fastening them securely with screws to the proper cleats and braces. Then take one of the boards intended for the sides and tack it so that the upper edge will be flush with the top of the end and center pieces. To accomplish this, it will be necessary to bend the bottom of the boat, thus obtaining the proper curve. The process is repeated on the opposite side, and the boat now begins to take shape.

While the boat is thus loosely fastened together, cut the center corner braces from the 1½ by 1½-in. stock, and the end braces from the 1½ by 3-in., and fit them as shown. After all the braces are in place, knock off the sideboards and cut gaskets of tar paper to fit every joint, then reassemble the boat piece by piece, tacking the tar paper gaskets, well coated with roofing cement, in each joint. In the final assembling of the boat it is best to use screws wherever possible, and to space the nails and screws not more than 2½ in. apart. After the final assembling,

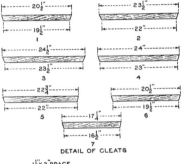

DETAIL OF CLEATS

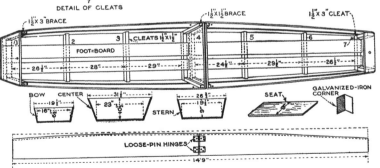

DIMENSIONS AND STRUCTURAL DETAIL FOR BUILDING THE TWO-SECTION ROWBOAT, THE HALVES OF WHICH CAN BE USED INDEPENDENTLY BY TWO INDIVIDUALS. THE HALVES OF THE BOAT ARE SECURED TOGETHER AT THE MIDDLE BY MEANS OF A LOOSE-PIN HINGES, FASTENED TO THE SIDES WITH STOVE BOLTS.

trim off the waste of the sideboards to fit the boat bottom. Then heat a quantity of roof cement and, while it is hot, run it into all cracks to ensure a watertight craft. When this done, fit the bow board, and the molding that forms the seat rail. The latter should be at least 5 in. from the top of the sides.

The footboards may next be laid; these are not essential, but make the boat stronger. Nail the galvanized-iron corners on the outside of the bow and stern, and the boat is ready to be cut into sections. Carefully saw between the centerboards until the two halves are separated, fit the hinges, using stove bolts instead of screws, and the boat is ready for use. If you wish to use an outboard motor with the boat, a 2-in. stern board should be used.

— A ROWBOAT GOES SAILING —

Any rowboat becomes a sailboat when equipped with this inexpensive portable sail rig. Although the dimensions given in *Figure 2* are for a small boat having a beam of 4 ft., the length of the thwart may be varied to suit the boat at hand. With the exception of the rudder and tiller, which should be made of oak, ¾ in. pine will do for the leeboards and thwart. Begin by making the thwart. Two pieces of 6-in. stock, cut to the proper length and mitered 22½ degrees, are held together with a notched cleat fastened to the underside with 1¼-in. brass screws as in *Figure 1*. The forward piece that rests on the breast hook is attached to the thwart with a large T-hinge. The barrel of the hinge should be fitted with a removable pin so that the assembly may be taken apart easily for storing. Two bolts passing through holes in the peak of the thwart securely

clamp the forward member in place. To make the rig adaptable for use on several boats whose beams may vary slightly, a series of ¼-in. holes spaced ¾ in. apart, is provided at each end of the thwart. These will be used for adjusting the two hook bolts that are bent from ¼-in. brass rod, threaded and fitted with wing nuts as in *Figure 3*. *Figure 4* shows how these bolts hook over the boat inwales.

Oak blocks are next bolted to the extreme ends of the thwart and are fitted with ⅜-in. bolts for attaching the leeboards as in *Figure 3*. Pieces of inner tube slipped over the bolts serve as rubber washers to keep the leeboards vertical. Strips of rubber, as well as rubber-headed tacks, are

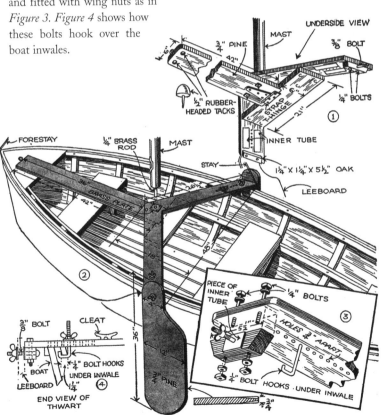

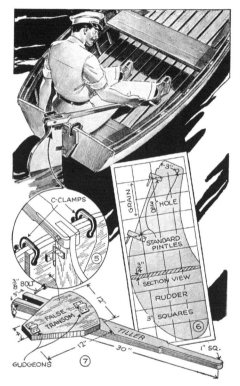

stock, following the design given in *Figure 2*. The after edge of the board is tapered as shown in the sectional detail. A 1/16 by 3 by 3-in. brass plate—with a ¼-in. hole made in the center to receive a brass pin driven up into the end of the mast—is screwed to the top side of the thwart at the center. The mast is held upright by two shrouds and a forestay. See *Figure 2*.

Details of the rudder, tiller, and false transom, and the method of clamping the assembly to the stern with a pair of C-clamps, are shown in *Figures 5, 6,* and *7*. Standard pintles and gudgeons are used to hinge the rudder, after which the

also fitted to the underside of the thwart to protect the finish of the boat. Next, the leeboards that provide lateral balance to the boat when under sail, are cut from 12-in. pine

tiller is pivoted at the top by a single bolt fitted with a wingnut. A small lanteen sail of 50 or 60 sq. ft. area, similar to a canoe or kayak sail, is recommended.

— SPEEDY KAYAK WITH LIGHT BUT STURDY FRAME —

Built by students in the Union High School at Newport Harbor, California, this graceful kayak has been awarded first prizes in competition. In building the boat, first make the stem and stern pieces, *A* and *M, Figure 3,* from ¾-in. white pine. These are rabbeted for the gunwales and strakes. Band-saw the ribs from 1⅛-in. white pine and fasten them along the keelson, assembling the frame over a simple form as shown in the photo under *Figure 2.* General dimensions and locations of frames are given in *Figure 1.* Use 1½-in. brass screws.

Follow with construction as shown in *Figure 4.* The uprights are attached to strips between gunwale and chine strake, instead of directly to the ribs. *Figure 5* shows location of strakes and deck strips. These members, as well as the keelson and gunwales, should have the edges rounded so that they will not change the canvas covering. A sectional view of the cockpit at rib *H* is shown in *Figure 6.* Aside from a light coaming, the

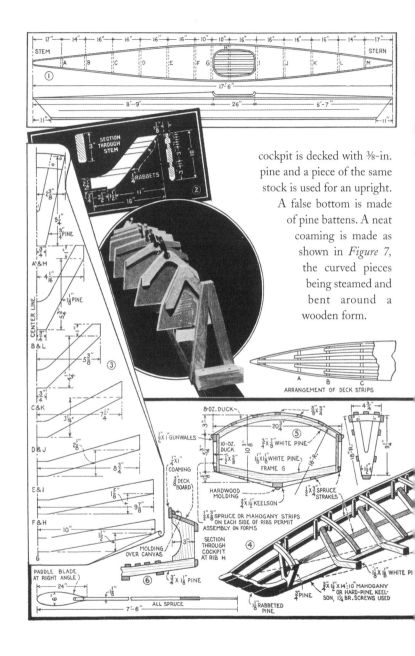

cockpit is decked with ⅜-in. pine and a piece of the same stock is used for an upright. A false bottom is made of pine battens. A neat coaming is made as shown in *Figure 7*, the curved pieces being steamed and bent around a wooden form.

ARRANGEMENT OF DECK STRIPS

To put on the 10-oz. bottom canvas, turn the frame upside down, stretch the fabric tightly, and tack it along the gunwales. The ends are lapped over the stem and stern as in *Figure 8*, marine glue first having been applied liberally under the seam. For the deck covering, use 8-oz. canvas. This is also tacked over

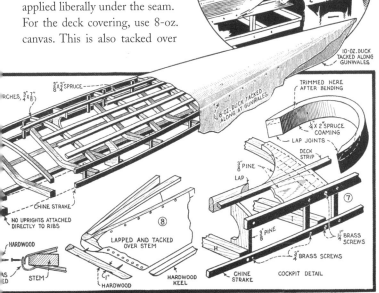

10-OZ. DUCK TACKED ALONG GUNWALES

¾" X ¾" SPRUCE

RCHES, ³¼" X ⅞")

8-OZ. DUCK TACKED ALONG AT GUNWALES

TRIMMED HERE AFTER BENDING

¾" X 2" SPRUCE COAMING

LAP JOINTS

DECK STRIP

⅝" PINE

LAP

CHINE STRAKE

NO UPRIGHTS ATTACHED DIRECTLY TO RIBS

⑧

⑦

⅝" PINE

1" BRASS SCREWS

HARDWOOD

LAPPED AND TACKED OVER STEM

STEM

HARDWOOD

¼" HARDWOOD KEEL

CHINE STRAKE

½" BRASS SCREWS

COCKPIT DETAIL

the gunwales. Use only copper or galvanized tacks, because iron tacks rust quickly and rot the canvas. The latter is tacked around the edges of the cockpit, the waste cut off, and the coaming completed. A light molding is installed around the coaming over the tacks, and an oak or mahogany molding around the gunwales.

One application of airplane wing dope is applied for a drum-tight waterproof job on the canvas. For paint, over this, use marine oil paint. If several coats are applied and allowed to dry, then sandpapered, a very smooth finish will result. Then apply the final color coats and finish the molding and coaming with a mahogany oil stain and spar varnish. The completed kayak weighs about 40 pounds.

— BUOYANT ONE-MAN POND RAFT —

When used as a boat or raft, an ordinary dry-goods box—even though it may be watertight—is unstable and readily tips due to its small size. However, by adding an old inner tube, as indicated in the illustration, this trouble is eliminated. Get a box that is large enough to sit in comfortably and about 20 in. deep. The boards should be tongue-in-groove stock if possible. Even then it will require two or possibly three coats of paint or preferably tar, to make the box watertight. Caulk the larger cracks first with tarred hemp or rope. After painting, stretch

ONE-MAN BOX CANOE
MADE BUOYANT WITH AUTO TUBE.

the inner tube around the box until it is about 8 in. below the upper edge. Then inflate the tube until it is round, except at the corners. Should the tube be too large to stay in place readily, tack small strips of wood just above it on all four sides. You will be surprised at the ease with which you can manipulate this raft without shipping any water.

— HOW TO BUILD A PADDLE-WHEEL BOAT —

This paddle-wheel boat was built in the spare time an outdoorsman and craftsman had on rainy afternoons and Saturdays, and the enjoyment derived from it at summer camp more than repaid the time spent on building. The materials used in its construction were:

  2 side boards, 14 ft. long, 10 in. wide, and ⅞ in. thick.

  2 side boards, 14 ft. long, 5 in. wide and ⅞ in. thick.

  1 outside keel board, 14 ft. long, 8 in. wide and ⅞ in. thick.

  1 inside keel board, 14 ft. long, 10 in. wide, and ⅞ in. thick.

120 sq. ft. of tongue-in-groove boards, ¾ in. thick, for bottom and wheel boxes.

1 piece timber, 2 in. square and 18 in. long.

4 washers.

2 iron cranks.

10 screw eyes.

30 ft. of rope

Nails.

THE BOAT AS IT APPEARS WITHOUT THE SPRING AND RUNNING BOARD AND USED AS A PLEASURE CRAFT OR FOR CARRYING FREIGHT, THE OPERATOR FACING IN THE DIRECTION OF THE BOAT'S TRAVEL.

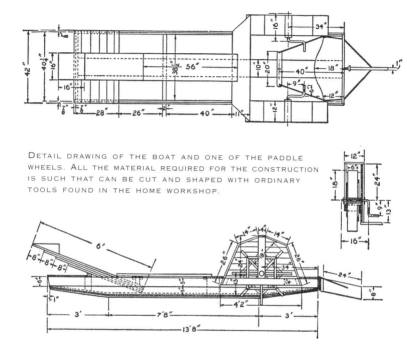

Detail drawing of the boat and one of the paddle wheels. All the material required for the construction is such that can be cut and shaped with ordinary tools found in the home workshop.

The dimensions given in the drawing will be found satisfactory, but these may be altered to suit the conditions. The first step is to cut and make the sides. Nail the two pieces forming each side together and then cut the end boards and nail them to the sides. Lay this framework, bottom side up, on a level surface and proceed to nail on the bottom boards across the sides. The ends of these boards are sawed off flush with the outside surface of the sides after they are nailed in place. The material list calls for tongue-in-groove boards for the bottom, but plain boards can be used, although it is then difficult to make the joint watertight. When the tongue-in-groove boards are used, a piece of string is well soaked in paint and placed in the groove of each board. This will be sufficient to make a tight joint.

Having finished the sides and bottom, the next step is to fasten on the bottom keel. Adjust the board to its position and nail it in the center part where it lies flat on the bottom boards. Then work toward the ends, gradually drawing it down over the turn and nailing it down. If the keel board cannot be bent easily, it is best to soak it in hot water where the bend takes place and the wood can then be nailed down without the fibers breaking. The inside keel is put on in the same manner, but reversed.

The next procedure is to make the paddle wheels. The hub for each wheel is made of a 2-in. square piece of timber, 9 in. long. Trim off the corners to make 8 sides to the piece, then bore a ¾-in. hole through its center. The 8 blades of each wheel, 16 in all, are 17 in. long, 6 in. wide, and ¾ in. thick. One end of each blade is nailed to one side of the hub, then it is braced as shown to strengthen the wheel.

The cranks are made of round iron, ¾ in. in diameter, and they are keyed to the wheels with large nails in the manner shown. A blacksmith shaped the cranks for the original boat, but if one has a forge the work can be done at home without that expense. The bearings for the crank-shafts consist of wood, although two large iron washers are preferable for this purpose. They should have a hole slightly larger than the diameter of the shaft, and drill holes in their rims so that they can be screwed to the wheel-box upright as shown. The bearings are lubricated with a little lard or grease.

The paddle-wheel boxes are built over the wheels with the dimensions given in the drawing, to prevent splashing water on the occupants of the boat.

The trimmings for the boat consist of three seats, a running board and a springboard. The drawings show the location of the seats. The springboard is built up of 4 boards, ¾ in. thick, as shown, only nailing them together at the back end. This construction allows the boards to slide over each other when a person's weight is on the outer end. The action of the boards is the same as a spring on a vehicle.

It is necessary to have a good brace across the boat for the back end of the springboard to catch on—a 2 by 4-in. timber being none too large. At the point where the springboard rests on the front seat there should be another good-sized crosspiece. The board can be held in place by a cleat and a few short pieces of rope, the cleat being placed across the board back of the brace. A little diving platform is attached on the outer end of the springboard and a strip of old carpet or gunny sack placed on it to prevent slivers from running into the flesh. In making the spring and running board, it is advisable to make them removable so that the boat can be used for other purposes.

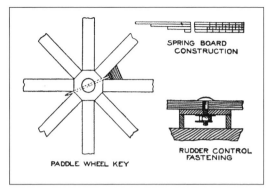

DETAIL OF PADDLE-WHEEL FASTENING, THE SPRINGBOARD CONSTRUCTION AND THE FASTENING FOR THE RUDDER CONTROL.

The boat is steered with a foot-operated lever, the construction of which is clearly shown. For the tiller-rope guides and rudder hinges, large screw eyes are used, the pin of the hinge being a large nail. The hull can be further strengthened by putting a few angle-iron braces either on the in or outside.

To make the boat watertight will require caulking by filling the cracks with twine and thick paint. The necessary tools are a broad, dull chisel and a mallet. A couple of coats of good paint, well brushed into the cracks, will help to make it watertight as well as shipshape. The boat may leak a little when it is first put into the water, but after a few hours of soaking, the boards will swell and close the openings.

This boat was used for carrying trunks, firewood, rocks, sand, and for fishing. And last, but not least, for swimming. The boat is capable of carrying a load of three-quarters of a ton. It draws very little water, thereby allowing its use in shallow water. It has the further advantage that the operator faces in the direction the boat is going, furnishing the power with his hands and steering with his feet.

— SEWING A SPLIT PADDLE —

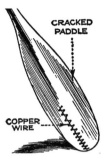

The split blade of a paddle or oar can be satisfactorily repaired by the simple process of sewing up the split with copper or brass wire. As a rule such a crack does not extend into the thick part of the blade and therefore the main consideration is to hold the edges of the crack securely together. To do this, punch or drill a series of small holes all along the crack, on both sides, about ¼ in. from the crack and ½ in. apart. The holes should be staggered, those on one side coming halfway between those on the other side. Clamp or bind the blade so that the crack will be tightly closed, and then sew it together by passing the wire through the holes, beginning at the point farthest from the tip of the blade. When the tip has been reached, work back again, using the same holes. Finish off by twisting the two ends and fastening them down with a copper tack or a small brass screw. Use No. 20 wire, and pull it tight at every stitch. Take care, however, not to break it at the sharp bends. As for the durability of such a repair, an oar repaired in this way has been used for an entire season without having any trouble at the seam. There are, of course, cases where this plan will not work. But in the majority of cases, where the edges are not broken apart on a long taper or bevel, the repair will be effective and permanent.

— FEATHERCRAFT GIVES NEW SPORT TO SWIMMERS —

Propelled half by swimming and half by paddling, these featherweight pontoons will provide plenty of sport at any beach. They are 6 ft. long, tapered and rounded at both ends. Top and bottom are pieces of ¾-in. white pine of exactly the same size and shape. These are screwed to nose and stern blocks and to two bulkheads located under the oarlock. Sides of 3/16-in. plywood are then cut out. It is best to use

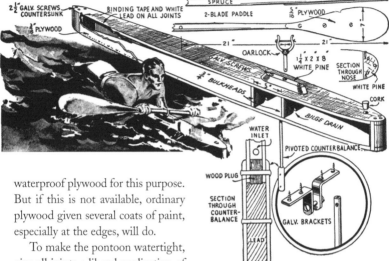

waterproof plywood for this purpose. But if this is not available, ordinary plywood given several coats of paint, especially at the edges, will do.

To make the pontoon watertight, give all joints a liberal application of oil-based paint and lay a strip of binding tape between the contacting surfaces. This should be done at the nose and stern blocks before the top and bottom are screwed on, and similarly when the plywood sides are attached.

Note the bilge drain in the bulkheads, which helps to empty the hull of water, should any get inside. The drain hole at the nose is corked when the pontoon is in use. Besides serving to drain out the water, the cork, if not pushed in too tight, will prevent the hull from bursting when the air inside expands under the hot sun, for which reason an air vent is necessary. A beveled block on the top

takes an oarlock for a two-blade paddle. To balance the pontoon properly, an 18-in. counterweight is pivoted to galvanized angle-iron brackets, which are screwed to the bottom directly under the oarlock.

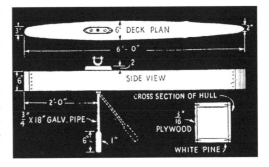

POWER PLAY

— A BOAT FOR YOUR OUTBOARD MOTOR —

The average rowboat is not entirely suitable for use with the outboard boat motor. The boat described in this article has been designed for the following: Perfect balance with the weight of the motor on the stern; a substantial stern and parts to carry the weight and hold up against vibration and strain; an easy riding bow that does not ship much water when the going is rough; large substantial seats; a front deck giving a motorboat appearance; light weight; ease of rowing, etc. The use of a motor on such a rowboat permits the builder to get into the motor-boat class to some extent, and a few of the refinements of the latter are embodied in the design. Although this par-

ticular boat has been designed especially for use with an outboard motor, the fundamentals of general rowboat practice have been closely followed.

The sides are two cypress boards, dressed on both sides. They are ⅞ in. thick, 16 in. wide, and 15 ft. 7 in. long, one to each side. You shouldn't have difficulty in obtaining these boards, but in some localities it may be necessary to make them up by using two boards; for instance, a 12- and a 4-in. width, doweled along the edges and clamped with a butt strap piece along the entire length. However, this type of construction is not recommended. The boards must be sawed to the shape indicated by the drawing so as to give the proper cur-

HERE IS A BOAT ESPECIALLY DESIGNED FOR THE OUTBOARD MOTOR, WHILE FOLLOWING CLOSELY GOOD PRACTICE IN MAKING A ROWBOAT.

vature to the bow and stern. If a band saw is available, the two boards can be shaped together readily; otherwise, you'll have to use a narrow saw and plane, doing the work by hand. Boards of this length will construct a boat 15 ft. long.

The stem piece is made of oak.

This wood lessens the danger of splitting and will furnish a substantial anchor for the screws used in attaching the sides. A piece of oak 3 in. thick, 6 in. wide and about 20 in. long is necessary. Two grooves are cut on the opposite sides, as shown in the drawing, to receive the ends of the side boards. Cut the top and bottom flush with the edges of the sides after they have been placed; it's best to do this just before the bottom boards are put on, so that a watertight joint may be assured.

The stern is of cypress, not less than 1½ in. thick. It may be necessary, although somewhat poor practice, to build the stern up of two widths. If you have to, splice along the joined edges with dowels and a longitudinal butt strap, as well as cross battens. A single width is much preferred.

The oak knees need be no particular shape, because they are simply braces. They should be about 2 in. in thickness, and used to strengthen the stem and stern. They are attached to the keelson and keel, preferably with bolts passing through these and the bottom. The knees cannot be set in place until the bottom, keelson, and keel have been put on. The general shape is indicated in the drawings, but may be altered to suit any special condition.

The battens consist of two cypress pieces, each 4 in. wide, dressed to ⅞-in. thickness. They run the full length of the side pieces, except for the thickness of the stern and the depth of the stem piece. Attach one batten along the inner lower side of each side board, to furnish additional bearing and screwing surface for the bottom boards.

After the sides have been carefully shaped, placed them side by side on their edges, top down. Cut 16 temporary crosspieces from scrap material, about 1½ in. wide and ⅞ in. thick; eight for the top spacing and eight for the bottom. Nail the bottom crosspieces to the side boards at their respective positions as indicated in the drawing (spacing arrangement). Turn the whole over so that it rests on the temporary crosspieces and nail on the top spacing pieces. When this has been done the sides will then assume their proper curvature. If there is any apparent lack of symmetry in the lines of the boat, you can adjust it by releasing the proper crosspieces and renailing.

The front ends of the sides should now be trimmed off and the stem piece inserted. If the fit is perfect, the sides should be permanently attached with screws. The stern is next fitted and the sides also attached with screws. The bottom is now put on, and the bottom temporary crosspieces should be removed one at a time, as the screwing on the bottom boards progresses.

The bottom is of cypress boards,

dressed to ⅞-in. thickness and about 10 in. in width. Attach these to the boat placing them across, and screw firmly in place. Position screws in the edges of the side and batten, alternately. The screws should be set in about 1 in. from the sides of the bottom boards and then spaced about 2 in. apart the rest of the distance across. The edges of the bottom boards and the side pieces should be fitted carefully so as to be parallel.

The keel and keelson are of the same size: 3 in. wide and ⅞ in. thick. However, the keelson, which runs the full length down the center of the inside bottom of the boat, is shorter than the keel. The keelson butts up against the inside of the stern and stem pieces and the knees rest upon it. The keel runs the full length of the outside from tip of stem to stern. The keelson and keel are held together through the bottom boards of the boat, with screws, copper rivets or bolts. Brass screws are satisfactory, in addition to small wood bolts about 3½ in. long, spaced about 12 in. apart along the entire length.

Place the midship thwart in position so as to give the boat more stability during the rest of the construction, after which the remaining temporary top cross spacers may be removed. The stern seat should be deep enough so that the operator can be seated while the motor is attached. The motor takes up a certain amount of inboard space and, in the average rowboat, the operator is compelled to sit to one side, resulting in an uneven balance. The rear seat should be low enough to allow plenty of clearance for the motor clamps. The bow seat should also be roomy, comfortable and low.

The deck may be arranged in any way desired. It should be somewhat higher at its inner end, so as to shed water. A cross or bulkhead piece is set across between the sides and used to support the deck. Two of these may be fitted if desired, one just aft of the stem piece.

All joints in the stern and stem assembly, along the bottom and between the bottom boards, should be made watertight. Carefully fit the surfaces in contact, and use a good make of marine glue between the surfaces before the parts are drawn up by screws. A piece of caulking cotton or any loosely woven material may be placed between the joints. The caulking cotton is best used in the stem and stern assembly and along the sides of the bottom, and you can fill the joints between the bottom boards simply with the marine glue. The screws draw the parts together and force out surplus glue, which, when set, will provide a boat that will stay dry for many seasons. However, unless built of very well seasoned lumber, no boat will stay tight if it is permitted to remain out of water and exposed to the rays of the hot summer sun.

Finish off the outside upper edge of the sides with a large half-round strip of molding, or a more elaborate coaming effect can be had by finishing with a flat strip around the top, projecting over the edge and filled in with a strip of quarter-round molding. Row locks should be set in the proper places, and brass rings attached

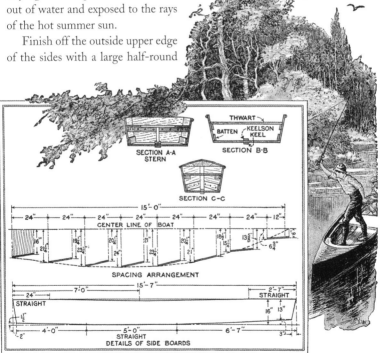

DETAILS OF CONSTRUCTION OF THE OUTBOARD-MOTOR BOAT. THIS CRAFT IS SIMPLE ENOUGH FOR ANY HANDYMAN TO BUILD, WITH ORDINARY TOOLS.

to the stem and stern. If desired, a small steering wheel can be placed in the bow with line running around the sides to the motor or rudder. The hardware used in assembling the boat may be of galvanized iron and such galvanized screws, bolts, etc., will serve very well. No excessive sizes are necessary.

The boat should be thoroughly painted. No attempt will be made here to describe any particular finish as every individual has his own ideas as to colors. At least two coats of oil primer should be given, followed by the top color coats that may be finished off with one or two coats of clear spar varnish. If a natural finish is desired, a coat of wood filler should be applied, followed by a shellac coat and two or three coats of good waterproof spar varnish.

— MOTORCYCLE-POWERED CATAMARAN —

A catamaran equipped with a stern paddle wheel and driven by an ordinary motorcycle is a craft particularly valuable in shallow water.

If a catamaran life raft is available, the expense of construction will be eliminated. However, it's not difficult to build one because it consists of a substantial wood frame decked with plank and covered with canvas. Additional buoyancy and seaworthiness are provided by airtight metal pontoons underneath each side, as shown in *Figure 1.* Openings must be provided in the deck, and suitable pieces incorporated in the frame, for supporting the power-transmitting rollers and the paddle wheel. All corners of the frame are strengthened with iron corner braces.

The pontoons are attached to the underside of the raft with iron hangers in the manner shown in *Figures 2 and 3.* The attachment of the pontoons completes the catamaran proper, and makes it ready to receive the rollers and other parts. These may be found among the materials, used and otherwise, that usually accumulate around the amateur's workshop. In any event, these parts are very easily obtained and comparatively inexpensive.

Bolt the wheel block, shown in *Figure 3,* to the center of the deck in such a manner that the front wheel of the motorcycle will be in line with the front edge of the deck. While an assistant holds the machine upright, take measurements for locating the

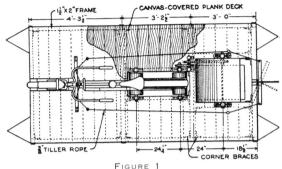

FIGURE 1

A MOTORCYCLE-DRIVEN CATAMARAN
THAT IS ESPECIALLY USEFUL IN
SHALLOW WATERS.

FIGURE 1 ILLUSTRATES HOW
POWER FROM THE MOTORCYCLE
ENGINE IS TRANSMITTED TO THE
PADDLE WHEEL.

FIGURE 2 SHOWS HOW THE AIR-
TIGHT PONTOONS ARE ATTACHED.

FIGURE 3, THE SIDE VIEW,
ILLUSTRATES THE METHOD OF
SUPPORTING THE MOTORCYCLE
AND HOW THE REAR WHEEL OF
THE MACHINE DELIVERS POWER
TO THE PADDLE WHEEL.

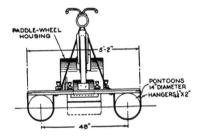

FIGURE 2

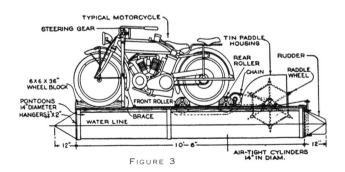

FIGURE 3

wooden rollers that support the rear wheel of the motorcycle and transmit the power of the engine to the paddle wheel. The bearings for the rollers are spaced just far enough apart so that, when the machine is installed as in *Figure 3,* the rear wheel will be the same height from the deck as the front one.

The locations of the rollers having been determined, the motorcycle is removed and the rollers and their bearings are ready to be attached. Both rollers are the same, with the exception that the rear roller has a gear wheel solidly attached to one end of its shaft. This gear meshes with a corresponding gear, immediately behind it, as shown in the detail, *Figure 4.* Referring to the detail, it will be seen that the latter gear is mounted on a short shaft, together with a sprocket wheel that should line up with the sprocket on the paddle wheel. This shaft is supported above the center of the gear on the rear roller by the bearing shown in the drawing. Both gear and sprocket wheels are solidly attached to the various shafts by means of pins or keys. Washers are provided on the shafts, between the rollers and their bearings, to prevent side play.

When the rollers and transmission gears have been attached, the opening in the deck is covered by a tin water shield that is attached underneath, as shown in *Figure 4,* to prevent water from splashing through.

The next step toward the completion off the craft is the paddle wheel, shown in detail in *Figure 5.* A roller similar to the ones described is provided, and a sprocket wheel for the driving chain is solidly attached to its shaft. The paddles are cut from heavy galvanized sheet iron. Bend one end of each blank paddle at right angles and punch or drill holes for attaching to the roller with screws.

As shown in the drawing, the paddles are separated from each other, and given strength and rigidity by iron braces that are attached with short bolts. The bolt holes of the paddle-wheel bearings are elongated, so that the paddle wheel may be moved back and forth to tighten or loosen the chain. Make a tin paddle housing and attach it to the deck, as shown in *Figure 3,* to prevent the revolving paddle from splashing water on the deck.

The motorcycle is held upright by an iron brace that clamps around the top bar of the machine. The lower ends are bolted to the deck. An extension at the upper end of this

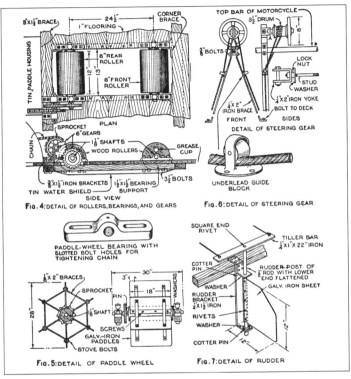

THE PARTS REQUIRED FOR THE CONSTRUCTION OF THE CATAMARAN ARE GENERALLY AVAILABLE AND INEXPENSIVE. FIGURES 4 TO 7 SHOW, IN DETAIL, THE CONSTRUCTION AND ASSEMBLY OF THE VARIOUS PARTS.

brace serves to carry the steering gear as shown in *Figure 6*. The steering wheel and the drum to which it is attached, are carried on a long stud that is secured with locknuts to a U-shaped iron yoke, as shown in the drawing. Holes are drilled through

the sides of the yoke, and a similar hole is drilled through the brace to accommodate a suitable bolt. A nut and washer hold the steering wheel and drum in place on the stud.

The remaining detail—a rudder for steering and maneuvering the craft—remains to be installed. Its essential details will be readily understood by reference to the detail in *Figure 7*. Bolt a simple rudder bracket of flat iron in the center of the stern. The iron rod that forms the rudderpost is held in place and prevented from pulling out by means of washers and cotter pins. The lower part of the rudderpost is filed flat and drilled for the attachment of the rudder proper, small bolts being used for the purpose. The rudder is cut from a piece of heavy galvanized sheet iron. The upper end of the rudderpost is squared off to fit into a corresponding square hole in the center of the tiller bar, to which it is riveted. Drill a hole in each end of the tiller bar for

attaching the tiller rope. This rope runs along the deck, on each side of the motorcycle, to the steering wheel on the brace. Suitable guide blocks of the underlead type are used for holding the rope in its proper location. No alterations of any kind are required on the motorcycle, which is controlled in the usual manner. You can remove the machine from the raft in just a few minutes if you want to ride it on land.

Various factors control the speed of such a craft, such as the size and weight of the raft and the power output of the motorcycle engine. But given an engine of good power, it is capable of making satisfactory speed in shallow water.

— HOW TO MAKE A HOUSEBOAT —

The houseboat shown is of the scow design, 6 ft. wide by 20 ft. long, with the cabin extending beyond the scow 1 ft. on each side. The scow tapers up at the forward end and is protected with a heavy sheet-iron plate so that the craft may be snubbed up on sandbars without danger of springing a leak, even

THE HULL OF THE HOUSEBOAT IS BUILT ON THE SCOW TYPE SO THAT IT CAN BE RUN IN SHALLOW WATER WITHOUT DANGER.

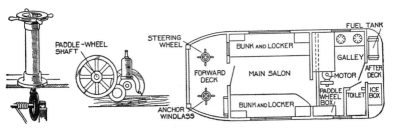

DETAIL OF THE ANCHOR WINDLASS AND ENGINE GEARING;
ALSO THE DECK PLAN, SHOWING THE LOCATION OF THE PARTS
AND THE ARRANGEMENT OF THE CABINS.

though a submerged log be struck while running at full speed. This boat is sturdy.

The power plant consists of a standard 4-hp. reversing gasoline engine that drives the paddles at their most efficient speed: 45 revolutions per minute through a 13-to-1 reduction. Cast-iron hubs, into which are inserted cold-rolled steel spokes and wood paddles bolted to their ends constitute the propeller wheels. The cruising speed is about 4 miles an hour.

Two wide bunks, beneath which is locker space, provide sleeping accommodations for a crew of four. In the kitchen the motor and gearing are almost completely concealed under the work table. The cooking is done on a two-burner blue-flame kerosene stove, and the sink is provided with running water suitable for washing dishes, etc. This water is drawn from a 30-gal. tank on the roof, which is filled by a centrifugal pump driven from the engine shaft. A modern toilet room is installed, and an ice chest on the after deck will hold supplies and ice for a week's cruise.

An acetylene-gas lighting system is installed and is used to light both cabins and a searchlight. A heavy anchor of special design is manipulated by a windlass on the forward deck. A similar device controls the rudder. Life rafts, complete with paddles, are placed on the roof. In hot weather these are moved to one end and an awning erected to make a cool sleeping place.

— Bracket to Attach Outboard Motor to a Canoe —

This simple bracket will enable you to attach an outboard motor to your canoe or kayak for swift transportation without arduous paddling. Outboard motors of ¾ to 2 hp. are sufficient for powering the average canoe. The bracket consists of a length of pipe fitted at one end with a hardwood block bolted in place to serve as a motor mount. L-hooks to fit under the gunwales attach the bracket to the boat.

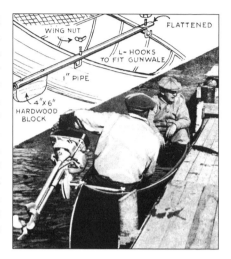

Floating Improvements

— Making a Drop Rudder —

There is nothing like a drop rudder for a sailing canoe or rowboat. And although it may seem difficult to rival a manufactured job, it is an easy matter to make one at much less cost, and that will answer the purpose just as well.

The material used is galvanized sheet iron. Stock of ¹/₁₆-in. thickness is heavy enough for the biggest boat on which such a rudder is likely to be used. The exact dimensions, shape and weight of the material depend, of course, on the size and model of the boat. Cut the blade to the shape indicated, making sure that it is perfectly straight, and then smooth the edges off nicely. The rudderpost is a length of ¼-in. flat steel, about 1½ in. wide. Rivet a wing piece to the lower part of this post as indicated, drilling a ½-in. hole through it in the center of the round end. Rivet the blade between the wings so that it can move up and down rather stiffly. The application of a little heavy oil or graphite grease will make it work with sufficient freedom without becoming too loose. The rivet may be a short piece of ½-in. steel rod or a short ½-in. bolt. A hole is also drilled in the blade to receive the rivet and it should be enlarged to about ¾ in. in diameter. File down a brass or iron washer, a trifle thicker than the blade, to a force fit in this hole and ream it out to fit on the rivet.

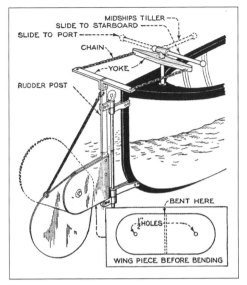

DETACHABLE DROP RUDDER FOR SAIL AND ROWBOATS.

To limit the downward swing of the blade, attach a length of furnace chain to the top and to the rudder post. To mount the rudder, the stern and rudder posts are fitted with eyes of flat steel, placed as indicated, so that the rudder cannot move up or down on the rod by which the assembly is held together. Removal of this rod allows the rudder to be taken off and lifted into the board when desired. The steering gear may consist either of a simple yoke of strap iron riveted to the rudderpost and moved by tiller ropes, or a double yoke, connected by chains and moved by a sliding tiller. The latter arrangement is more "shipshape."

If the boat has a curved stern, curve the rudderpost to correspond, except for that part to which the wing piece is attached. The locking rod must, of course, also be curved. The lower rudder and stern post must then be attached immediately above the wing piece.

— NOVEL BOAT HOIST —

Where a great many boats or canoes are kept, a boat hoist of the kind shown in the drawing will prove very useful. The hoist is made of 4 by 4-in. lumber and consists of a cradle, which is submerged to that the boat can be driven over it, and a lever, which extends vertically from the cradle and is pulled down to raise the cradle above the surface of the water. To permit this, the hoist must be pivoted on the edge of the dock as indicated. The pivot is a ¾- or ⅝-in. iron rod extending through the frame and also through two 4 by 4-in. blocks, securely bolted to the dock. A rope is attached to the top of the lever so that it can be readily pulled down. A large screw eye is driven into the dock for fastening the rope.

CONVENIENT HOIST FOR RAISING ROWBOATS AND CANOES IS ATTACHED
TO THE DOCK AND CAN EASILY BE OPERATED BY ONE MAN.

SCRAPING THE BOAT IN PREPARATION FOR WATERPROOFING, MELTING THE GLUE AND APPLYING IT TO THE HULL WITH A WIRE SINK BRUSH.

— HOW TO MAKE YOUR BOAT WATERTIGHT —

This simple method makes old and leaky boats and canoes as good as new at small cost.

There is nothing more annoying, upon reaching the summer camp on the lake or river, than to find the canoe or boat, after its long storage during the winter, gaping at the seams and ready to go to the bottom as soon as it is launched. Or to embark on a fishing trip, after looking the boat over and deciding that it will do all right, and then spend the better part of the day in laborious bailing instead of fishing. The usual remedy is to sink the craft in shallow water and wait until the wood swells and closes the seams. But although this will work in a majority of the cases, the owner is deprived of the use of the boat for a period of several precious days.

The hull, of course, can be caulked. But after this is done, the owner is very likely to have the whole job to do over again next season, thus wasting more time. There is a way, however, to get rid of the annual overhaul or wetting of the boat, or the continuous bailing. It is a way that will ensure a dry boat not only this season but next, and the season after that, with no more work to be done after the first job. Boats treated in this manner have been known to stand up for twenty years without further attention, and without necessitating the bailing of a single drop of water other than that deposited in them by the rain. The hull is also considerably stiffened, a factor of decided importance when an outboard motor is used. This can increase the useful life of the boat by years.

This method of waterproofing a boat demands no expert knowledge,

and is not expensive. The only things needed are a supply of marine glue sufficient to cover the boat properly, some cotton cloth, a kerosene stove to heat the glue, a brush, some tacks and a hammer, and some old flat-irons. The marine glue used should be Jeffrey's No. 7 black, soft marine glue, or special marine canoe glue, according to the type of the craft. One pound of the glue will water-proof 3 sq. ft. of surface, so it is nec-essary to figure the area of the hull to get the correct amount to order. The cloth used should be heavy, unbleached cotton cloth, of a firm, close weave, which can be obtained at any dry goods store. It must be purchased in one length, wide enough to cover one side of the boat completely, allowing for all curves, and a yard or two more than twice as long as the boat. It is cut in two, and each length used to cover one side of the boat.

If the boat is clinker-built (lap-staked), it is wise to cover the whole side, carrying the cloth to the gun-wale. If the boat is carvel-built (smooth-sided), it will only be nec-essary to carry the cloth a few inches above the waterline. First, scrape all the loose paint from the hull and remove all dirt and oil. Then remove the stem band at the bow and, starting from the stern, stretch the cloth over one side of the boat, tacking it to the transom and the bow. Do the same with the other side, using ½-in. copper tacks, and allow the cloth to remain on the hull for about 24 hours. This stretches the cloth and makes it conform somewhat to the shape of the hull. When stretching, see that there are no slack places in the cloth. After the time specified, remove the cloth pieces and mark them for their respective sides.

Now melt the marine glue in any kind of suitable container over the stove, using a moderate flame and stirring it frequently. If a kerosene stove is not at hand, the glue can be melted over a small fire, but care must be taken that the flame is not too hot, because the glue must not be allowed to boil. The glue should be cut into small pieces before melting, and it should be carefully watched until it will drip from the stirring paddle like oil, at

which point it is ready for use. It must be used as promptly as possible, and it must be liquid when used or it will not fill the seams properly. Apply it with a wire sink brush or, failing this, with the stub of a small whiskbroom. Whichever, the tool must be stiff and well bound. Apply a heavy coat to the entire surface to be covered.

Now tack the end of one piece of canvas to the stern of the boat and start drawing it tightly toward the

METHOD OF COVERING SEAMS WHERE ENTIRE BOAT IS NOT TO BE COVERED.

STRETCHING THE CLOTH OVER
THE HULL, IRONING IT DOWN,
AND THE LAST STEP,
PAINTING THE BOAT.

other end. Draw it as tight as possible and tack at the bow. Next tack along the gunwale, stretch, and tack along the keel. If the cloth is wetted before applying, it can be stretched more easily and, when it shrinks, it will hug the hull more closely. However, if it is wet, take care that it is thoroughly dry before the next operation.

The next step is to iron the cloth down into close contact. Do this with either a flatiron or a gasoline or electric iron, which can be cleaned afterward with gasoline. The application of the hot iron causes the glue to sweat through the cloth. The iron must not be used as in ironing clothes but rather with a wobbling motion, on its own axis, and it must be passed in this manner over the entire surface of the cloth until the cloth is black. The operations on the other side of the boat are, of course, exactly similar to this. The iron must not be too hot, because this will prevent the cloth from sticking to the hull. A little experimenting will enable you to determine the proper heat.

Allow no excess of glue to remain on the surface of the cloth, because this will later "bleed" through the paint. The cloth from both sides must lap over the entire width of the keel, and be perfectly ironed down—similarly at the bow. The cloth must lap over the stern piece or transom about 1 in. and be well ironed down also. Trim off all rough edges and overhanging lengths of cloth.

Now cut two pieces of the cloth about 2 in. wide, and long enough to reach from the keel to the gunwale along the joint between the side boards and the transom. Tack along the joint, allowing 1 in. on each side, then iron down into place. Feel all over the bottom of the boat for lumps caused by a little too much glue, and iron these down smooth.

If the boat is clinker-built, the cloth need only be trimmed at the gunwale and tacked neatly. But if it is carvel-built, and the cloth has been carried only to a point a few inches above the waterline, get some twilled tape and proceed as follows: Trim off the rough edges of the cloth with a sharp knife parallel with the gunwale. Then tack down the tape along the line so that it covers the rough edge. This will make a joint that will hardly be noticed when the boat is painted. Iron down the tape in the same manner as the cloth; there will usually be enough glue on the hull to permit this without applying any more.

After ironing, apply one or two coats of orange shellac to the entire hull, to prevent the glue from discoloring the paint. When the shellac is dry, paint the boat. Any good paint can be used for the purpose, and if a good finish is desired, the last coat should be well rubbed down with pumice and linseed oil. Finally, apply two coats of good spar varnish. This last operation should be done in a warm room, free from dust.

When an old boat is being waterproofed, the keel and stem pieces should be removed if possible, until the process is complete. When replacing them, they should be set in marine glue to avoid leaks at the screw holes.

If you desire to cover only the seams of a boat, proceed as shown in the small drawing. Melt the glue as before, and only as much as is required for immediate use. Because it is used from the melting pot more can be added from the can. Apply a heavy coat to the seams, spreading it on either side of them for about 1½ or 2 in. Stretch strips of unbleached cotton over the seams and tack in place, then apply the iron and finish the job in the manner already described.

These instructions cover only one type of boat, but they apply, with minor modifications, to all types. Of course, you may vary them to suit your own boat. For example, on a flat-bottom boat with no keel it is feasible to apply the cloth in one piece, although it may be found more difficult to get a smooth job. If the job is done with care, a boat waterproofed in this manner will last a lifetime. Any small holes that it may acquire later in service can be patched in a half hour by the same methods.

— NONDRAGGING ANCHOR FOR SMALL BOATS —

Prices for anchors used to hold small mooring buoys seemed so exorbitant that a boater decided to make one at a fraction of the cost. He got several 2-ft. lengths of ½-in. iron rod from a dumping ground, and bent the ends over as shown. Then he forced these rods through a sack of ordinary

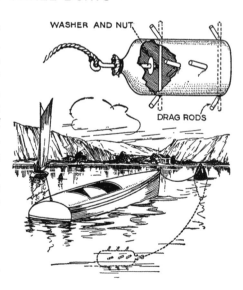

WASHER AND NUT

DRAG RODS

NONDRAGGING ANCHOR
FOR SMALL MOTORBOAT
MADE FROM SACK OF
CEMENT AND IRON RODS.

cement and turned the ends toward the mouth of the sack. Another rod of the same length was threaded at one end, a large washer slipped on, and a nut then screwed on to keep the washer in place. He bent the other end to form an eye through which the anchor line was slipped and tied. This rod was pushed into the bag of cement with the eye extending outside of the mouth as shown. The cement was hosed with water and left to harden overnight. The result was as good an anchor as could be purchased, and it cost only the price of the cement.

— ANCHORS FOR SMALL-BOAT LANDING —

The drawing shows a novel method of using cement blocks to anchor a small boat landing. The blocks are made in a rectangular shape and of a size depending on the width of the landing. A block 8 by 8 by 20 in. in dimensions was found to be a convenient size. Lengths of ½-in. flat iron are set into the ends of the blocks while the cement is soft, the exposed portion of each piece being rounded to form a ring that fits the pile loosely.

In setting up the framework of the landing, the piles on one side are the first driven in. The rings at one end of

CEMENT BLOCKS USED TO ANCHOR SMALL BOAT LANDING. THEY ARE LOCATED BETWEEN THE PILES.

the blocks are placed over the piles and the blocks are lowered down to the bottom. The blocks are then shifted to the correct position and the other piles located in the rings and driven down about 2 ft. Crosspieces, nailed to the piles at their upper ends, and two long 2 by 12-in. timbers, nailed along them as shown, form the framework upon which 2-in. lumber is nailed to form a walk.

— AN IMPROVISED FERRY —

A camping party selected a campsite near the bank of a narrow but deep stream. A farmhouse was located on the other side of the stream, and this was the nearest place where the camping party could obtain fresh food supplies such as butter, milk and eggs.

To avoid going around to the nearest bridge, and also to avoid the tiresome task of rowing over the stream, a simple ferry was improvised in the following way: The campers hired a small boat and fitted a rudder about three times the usual size to it. They rigidly stretched a heavy wire between two strong posts on opposite sides of the stream and a sheathed pulley was run on this wire. The boat was attached to the pulley by means of a rope about 30 ft. long, the bow pointing upstream. The boat could

A NOVEL METHOD OF USING A ROWBOAT TO FERRY ACROSS A STREAM.

then easily be moved from side to side by manipulating the rudder, which, when set to the left, caused the boat to move toward the right and vice versa. Although the velocity of the stream was not very great, it only took about three minutes to cross it, a distance of approximately 120 feet.

— Flat Boat Inverted over Oil Drum Provides Handy Diving Board —

While vacationing at an inland lake where there was no diving board at hand, the members of a camping party inverted an old flat boat over an oil drum, which was sealed tightly. The drum supported one end of the boat above water so it served nicely as a temporary diving board.

— Improvements for a Fishing Boat —

A tackle box fitted in the seat of a rowboat has many advantages over an ordinary tackle box, because it has much more room and cannot be knocked around, and is also kept completely out of the way. As shown in the drawing, the tackle box is made in the form of a drawer under the center seat, the one that is usually used the most. The drawer is about 30 in. long, 6½ in. deep, and 12 in. wide. This leaves plenty of room for two or three rods, and compartments for hooks and lures, so that these will not become mixed

LEFT: Making a slat floor for the fishing boat.
RIGHT: Tackle box built under seat.

as is generally the case in the ordinary tackle box. The box is protected from rain by the seat, and because it does not touch the bottom it is also free from water in the boat. A hasp and padlock should be provided on the box.

Another improvement for the boat is a slat flooring to prevent getting the feet wet. For convenience, the flooring can be arranged in three sections. The construction is simple, all that is necessary being a quantity of slats and a few cross members. The best wood to use is fir, and the flooring should never be painted, but should be given a liberal application of linseed oil. The slats, so protected, will last a long time. In addition to keeping the feet dry, the slat flooring protects the bottom boards of the boat.

— ANCHOR CHAIN HELPS DIVER CLIMB INTO BOAT FROM WATER —

When using a rowboat as a diving platform, difficulty getting into the boat from the water can be overcome by using the anchor chain as a step. The step can be made any height desired by using a screw hook to fasten it as indicated. A length of garden hose slipped over the chain will provide a cushion for the feet.

— ❖ ❖ ❖ —

{ CHAPTER 5 }

THE
REMARKABLE
MARKSMAN

THE WOODSMAN ARCHER

— MAKING TACKLE —

Whether you try to land six in the gold for a perfect fifty-four or take your archery with a dash of small-game hunting, you will find keen enjoyment in this ancient sport. Making the tackle is simple.

SIZE OF TACKLE: The first thing to know is what size of bow and length of arrow to use. This depends entirely on your physique, and particularly your reach. If your reach is 64 in., you can use an arrow 25 to 26 in. long, with a bow not less than 5 ft. 3 in. from tip to tip, *Figure 5*. The weight of the bow, that is, the number of pounds pull required to draw it, depends on your muscular development. Most men can draw a 50- to 60-pound bow, but a 35- to 40-pound bow is the best weight for general shooing, and good scores can be made with the 25 and 30 pounders.

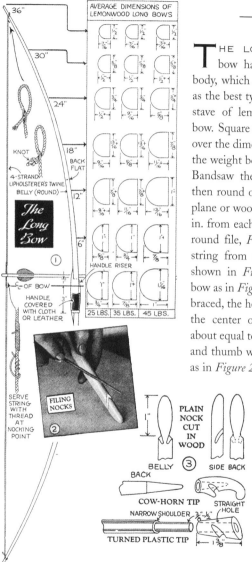

AVERAGE DIMENSIONS OF LEMONWOOD LONG BOWS

HANDLE RISER

| 25 LBS. | 35 LBS. | 45 LBS. |

The Long Bow

4-STRAND UPHOLSTERER'S TWINE BELLY (ROUND)

KNOT

BACK FLAT

C OF BOW
HANDLE COVERED WITH CLOTH OR LEATHER

SERVE STRING WITH THREAD AT NOCKING POINT

FILING NOCKS ②

PLAIN NOCK CUT IN WOOD

BELLY ③ SIDE BACK
BACK

COW-HORN TIP STRAIGHT HOLE
NARROW SHOULDER

TURNED PLASTIC TIP

— BOWS —

THE LONG BOW: The long bow has a deep or "stacked" body, which is generally recognized as the best type of bow shape. Use a stave of lemonwood for the long bow. Square up the stave to a little over the dimensions at the handle of the weight bow you intend to make. Bandsaw the wood, *Figure 4,* and then round off the belly side with a plane or wood rasp. Cut the nocks 1 in. from each end, *Figure 3,* using a round file, *Figure 2.* Make a bow-string from upholsterer's twine, as shown in *Figure 1,* and brace the bow as in *Figure 6.* When the bow is braced, the height of the string from the center of the bow should be about equal to the width of the hand and thumb with the latter stuck out as in *Figure 28.* You can now "tiller" it to check the bend of both limbs, at the same time measuring the weight with a spring scale, as shown in *Figure 10.*

Bend the bow gradually. Take off a shaving here and there to equalize the bend. Take your

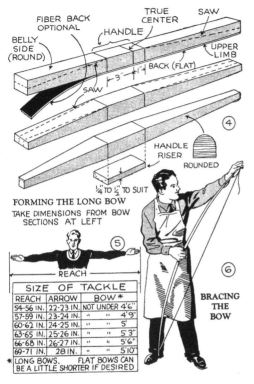

FIBER BACK OPTIONAL

BELLY SIDE (ROUND)

HANDLE

TRUE CENTER

SAW

UPPER LIMB

BACK (FLAT)

SAW

—3"—|—1"—|

④

HANDLE RISER

ROUNDED

¼ TO ½ TO SUIT

FORMING THE LONG BOW
TAKE DIMENSIONS FROM BOW
SECTIONS AT LEFT

⑤

←—— REACH ——→

⑥

BRACING THE BOW

SIZE OF TACKLE		
REACH	ARROW	BOW*
54-56 IN.	22-23 IN.	NOT UNDER 4'6"
57-59 IN.	23-24 IN.	" " 4'9"
60-62 IN.	24-25 IN.	" " 5'
63-65 IN.	25-26 IN.	" " 5'3"
66-68 IN.	26-27 IN.	" " 5'6"
69-71 IN.	28 IN.	" " 5'10"

*LONG BOWS. FLAT BOWS CAN BE A LITTLE SHORTER IF DESIRED

string cuts the center of the belly, as in *Figure 7*. If it throws off to the side, your bow has a turn in it. This can be corrected by taking off wood opposite the turn.

If desired, you can back your bow with red or black fiber attached with waterproof glue before the shaping is started. Instead of cutting plain nocks, you may decide to purchase and fit a set of cowhorn tips or you may want to turn them from colorful plastic. It will be noted, *Figure 3*, that plain nocks are not cut across the back of the bow as this would weaken the wood. The groove in horn or plastic tips, however, is let into the back.

THE FLAT BOW: The flat bow is easier to make than the long one and can be 3 or 4 in. shorter for the same length arrow. The same general method of bandsawing is used, *Figure 8*, but the belly side is

time. You can always take off more wood, but you can't put it back on again. The bow should be quite stiff for a distance of about 6 in. at the center, and should then curve evenly to the tips. The beginner's most common fault is to make the bow "whip ended," *Figure 9*. Besides checking the curvature, sight down the bow as you work and note if the

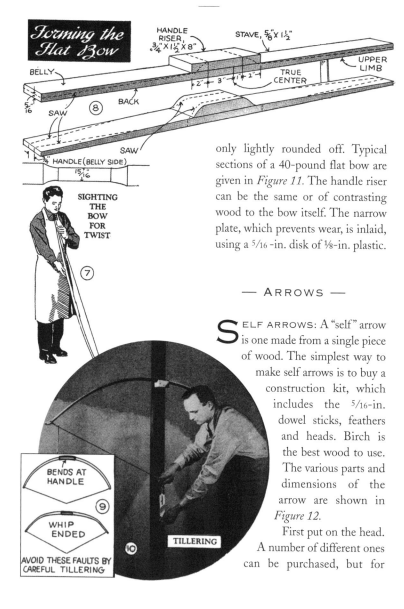

Forming the Flat Bow

HANDLE RISER, 3/4" X 1 1/2" X 8"

STAVE, 5/8" X 1 1/2"

UPPER LIMB

BELLY

BACK

TRUE CENTER

2' — 3" — 1" — 2'

5/16"

SAW

⑧

1/4" HANDLE (BELLY SIDE)

15/16"

SAW

SIGHTING THE BOW FOR TWIST

⑦

BENDS AT HANDLE

⑨

WHIP ENDED

AVOID THESE FAULTS BY CAREFUL TILLERING

TILLERING

⑩

only lightly rounded off. Typical sections of a 40-pound flat bow are given in *Figure 11.* The handle riser can be the same or of contrasting wood to the bow itself. The narrow plate, which prevents wear, is inlaid, using a 5/16-in. disk of 1/8-in. plastic.

— ARROWS —

SELF ARROWS: A "self" arrow is one made from a single piece of wood. The simplest way to make self arrows is to buy a construction kit, which includes the 5/16-in. dowel sticks, feathers and heads. Birch is the best wood to use. The various parts and dimensions of the arrow are shown in *Figure 12.*

First put on the head. A number of different ones can be purchased, but for average target work the brass parallel pile head is most satisfactory. Cut the tenon on the end of the shaft by turning on a lathe, *Figure 14.* If you are careful, the head will be a drive fit and will hold securely. If the head is a bit loose, anchor it with a few punch taps as shown in *Figure 16.* Cut the arrows to the required length and then cut the nocks. Plain nocks can be cut easily by running the shafts over a circular saw, as in *Figure 13.* The nock should be across the grain. If you want more strength at the nock, insert a thin slip of fiber or plastic. Aluminum or molded-plastic nocks are very attractive and are fitted by tenoning the end of the shaft the same as in fitting the head.

Fletching is the hard part of arrow making. However, if you use one of the jigs shown in *Figures 17 and 19,* you will be able to turn out good work at a fair rate of speed. Turkey

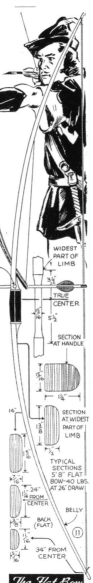

ARROW PLATE

WIDEST PART OF LIMB

3½

TRUE CENTER

5/16 5½

SECTION AT HANDLE

15/16 1¼

14″ 13/8 SECTION AT WIDEST PART OF LIMB

TYPICAL SECTIONS 5′8″ FLAT BOW—40 LBS. AT 26″ DRAW

5/16 7/16 24″ 1½ FROM CENTER

BELLY

3/8 BACK (FLAT)

1½/16 5/16 34″ FROM CENTER

The Flat Bow

feathers can be purchased already cut, or you can strip your own feathers by grasping the vane at the tip and pulling outward, as shown in *Figure 15,* afterward cutting the vane to the required shape.

The one-feather fletching jig shown in *Figures 17 and 18* is built around a paper clip. A disk of plywood, which slips over the shaft, is drilled with three small holes to supply an indexing head, and is prevented from slipping by means of a piece of spring wire. One feather at a time is clamped by the paper clip and pressed into position.

Any type of adhesive can be used. Celluloid cement has the advantage of quick drying and the ability to anchor on lacquer, thus allowing the shafts to be painted

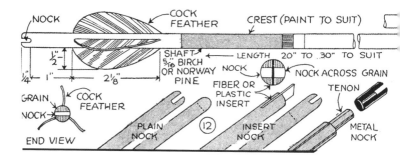

NOCK • COCK FEATHER • CREST (PAINT TO SUIT)

SHAFT
5/16 BIRCH OR NORWAY PINE • LENGTH 20" TO 30" TO SUIT

NOCK • FIBER OR PLASTIC INSERT • NOCK ACROSS GRAIN • TENON

1/2" • 1/4" • 1" • 2 1/8"

GRAIN • COCK FEATHER • NOCK • END VIEW

PLAIN NOCK • 12 • INSERT NOCK • METAL NOCK

previous to fletching. Waterproof glue on bare wood is the most durable. In the three-feather jig, the feathers are held between metal plates, one plate of each set fitting into grooves in the top and bottom members. The upper ring is removable, being a press fit over the three spacing dowels.

FOOTED ARROWS: Footed arrows are more decorative and more durable than self arrows. The footing is made from any tough hardwood,

CUTTING NOCKS

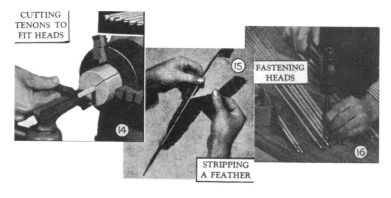

CUTTING TENONS TO FIT HEADS

FASTENING HEADS

STRIPPING A FEATHER

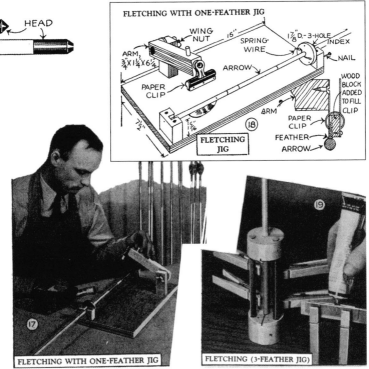

FLETCHING WITH ONE-FEATHER JIG

FLETCHING (3-FEATHER JIG)

and is slotted for a distance of 5¼ in., *Figure 20*. Shafts are usually Port Orford cedar or Norway pine, and are tapered to fit the slot in the footing. Perfect tapering of the shafts can be done by the circular-saw method shown in *Figures 21* and *24*. The taper should be made with the flat of the grain. The shaft is assembled to the footing with waterproof glue and the assembly is then clamped or wrapped with twine or rubber strips as in *Figure 22*. Other than a special tenoning jig, the best method of rounding the footing to match the rest of the shaft is by turning, *Figure 23*. Nocks for footed arrows are usually of the same wood as used for the footing. The insert is let into the end of the shaft, and is later rounded off and grooved in the usual manner.

ACCESSORIES: If you want to

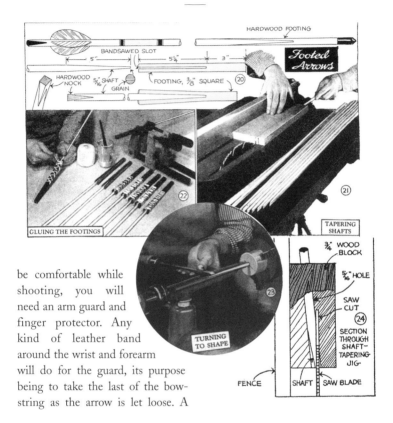

be comfortable while shooting, you will need an arm guard and finger protector. Any kind of leather band around the wrist and forearm will do for the guard, its purpose being to take the last of the bow-string as the arrow is let loose. A

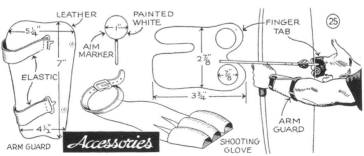

simple finger tab of soft leather shaped as shown in *Figure 25* will provide protection for your fingers, or you may prefer to make or buy a three-finger shooting glove. An excellent target can be made by cementing four or five layers of corrugated cardboard together, painting the rings directly on the cardboard or on a piece of oilcloth. A simple target stand is made from ¾-in. lumber, as shown in *Figure 27.*

— STANCE FOR SHOOTING —

Stand with your feet well apart, left side facing the target, as shown in *Figures 26* and *29.* Hold the bow horizontal and fit an arrow across the arrow plate. Grasp the arrow with the thumb or first finger of the left hand, *Figure 30,* and with the right hand twirl the arrow until the cock feather is perpendicular to the bowstring. Adjust your grip on the string, as shown at the right in *Figure 25,* and start the draw. Pull back slowly until your right

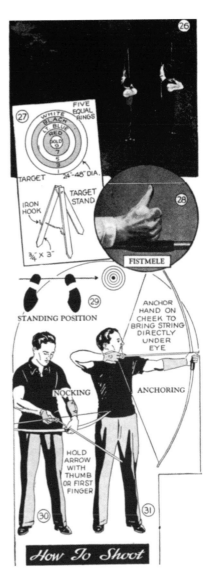

FIVE EQUAL RINGS
WHITE · BLACK · LT. BLUE · RED · GOLD
TARGET 24"-48" DIA.
TARGET STAND
IRON HOOK
¾" X 3"
FISTMELE
STANDING POSITION
NOCKING
ANCHORING
ANCHOR HAND ON CHEEK TO BRING STRING DIRECTLY UNDER EYE
HOLD ARROW WITH THUMB OR FIRST FINGER
How To Shoot

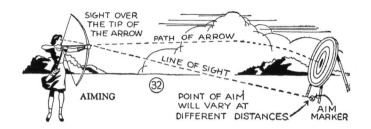

SIGHT OVER THE TIP OF THE ARROW

PATH OF ARROW

LINE OF SIGHT

AIMING

POINT OF AIM WILL VARY AT DIFFERENT DISTANCES

AIM MARKER

hand comes to a fixed "anchor" point on your jawbone, *Figure 31*. In this position, the string should be under and in line with the right eye. Aiming is done by sighting over the tip of the arrow to some fixed point previously determined as the correct point of aim at the distance being shot. *Figure 32* illustrates this method of aiming.

— SIGHT ON ARCHERY BOW IMPROVES AIM —

Taped to your archery bow, this adjustable sight will be found a more satisfactory method of shooting an arrow than the "point-of-aim" method, because you aim right at the bull's-eye instead of sight-ing at a marker on the ground in front of the target. Thus, any variation in bowing or in distance is not likely to affect your aim. The parts of the sight are made of heavy sheet steel or brass and are cut to the shape and sizes given in the detail. When finished, they should be polished with fine emery cloth or steel wool. Nickel or chromium plating will improve their appearance. The sight is mounted on the back of the bow with the sight end of the cross bar extending to the left. It is adjustable either vertically or horizontally. Once set for a certain shooting distance, the sight may be marked so that when the same distance is shot again, the correct adjustment can be made without any trouble.

— MAKING ARROWS VISIBLE —

To locate your archery arrows easily after shooting them, wrap bands of tinfoil on the shafts just in front of the feathers, and shellac the bands to prevent tearing. The tinfoil will glisten in the sun so that an arrow can be seen at a distance of many yards. This method is especially effective in cases where the arrows happen to fall in tall grass, weeds, etc.

— A VERSATILE HOMEMADE BOW SIGHT —

This simple, lightweight device has all the adjustable variations of an expensive bow sight, and with an average-weight bow is fairly accurate for distances well over 100 yards. Cut from a strip of cork gasket material 1 in. wide by 6 in. long, the sight is fastened with adhesive tape to the back of the bow just above the leather grip. After gluing the cork in place, put a strip of cellulose tape on the belly of the bow opposite the cork. Stick a 2-in. round-bead hat pin into the cork so that the head projects ½ in. beyond the left edge of the bow. Then, by the trial-and-error

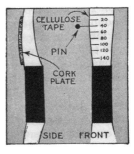

method at various distances, determine the proper position of the pin for each distance and mark these positions in ink on the tape, numbering them accordingly. A coat of clear shellac will protect both the cork and the scale.

— BAMBOO BOW AND ARROW —

STRONG, DURABLE BOWS AND ARROWS
CAN BE MADE FROM BAMBOO FISHING POLES.

Almost every boy, at some time or other, would like to try his skill with a bow and arrow. But it is rather difficult to obtain a satisfactory piece of wood for the bow. Seasoned hickory is usually recommended, but an excellent substitute is the bamboo from a cheap fishing pole. With reasonable care, a 5-ft. length of bamboo may be split into pieces of small dimensions; twelve or fifteen being obtained from a pole 1½ in. in diameter.

After splitting it, the pieces of heart or hardened pith at the joints should be removed with a knife or plane so that the strips can be bound together in a compact bundle. The binding is a very particular part of the work if the bow is to be made serviceable for any considerable length of time, and waxed cord should be used for this purpose. To begin, bind the middle section of the bundle to a distance of 6 in. on either side of the exact center.

After fastening the string ends, cut away one-fourth of the number of sticks in the bundle just beyond the wrapping, and bind those remaining at points about 16 in. from the center of the bow. Cut away as many sticks as before and bind again, proceeding in this way until one-fourth of the sticks of the bundle remain. These are bound at the tip ends, and the bow is ready to receive the string.

If the work has been done carefully, the result will be a well-balanced bow that will last for years, especially if the bowstring is loosened after using it so that the bamboo may straighten again and retain its elasticity. Serviceable arrows may also be made of similar material by binding four of the narrow strips together and inserting balancing feathers.

— HOW TO MAKE A CROSSBOW AND ARROW SLING —

It is best to use maple for the stock in making this crossbow. But if this wood cannot be procured, good straight-grained pine will do. The material must be 1½ in. thick, 6 in. wide and a trifle over 3 ft. long. The bow is made from straight-grained oak, ash, or hickory, ⅝ in. thick, 1 in. wide and 3 ft. long. A piece of oak, ⅜ in. thick, 1½ in. wide and 6 ft. long, will be sufficient to make the trigger, spring and arrows. A piece of tin, some nails and a good cord will complete the materials necessary to make the crossbow.

The piece of maple or pine selected

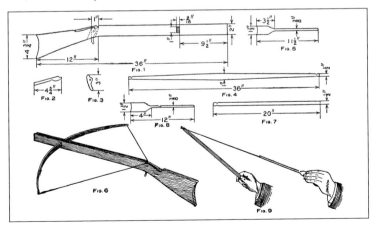

DETAILS OF THE BOW-GUN AND ARROW SLING.

for the stock must be planed and sandpapered on both sides then marked and cut as in *Figure 1*. A groove is cut for the arrows in the top straight edge ⅜ in. wide and ⅜ in. deep. The tin is bent and fastened on the wood at the back end of the groove where the rod slips out of the notch; this is to keep the edges from splitting.

A mortise is cut for the bow at a point 9½ in. from the end of the stock, and one for the trigger 12 in. from the opposite end, which should be slanting a little as shown by the dotted lines. A spring, *Figure 2*, is made from a good piece of oak and fastened to the stock with two screws. The trigger, *Figure 3*, which is ¼ in. thick, is inserted in the mortise in the position when pulled back, and adjusted so as to raise the spring to the proper height. Then a pin is put through both stock and trigger, having the latter swing quite freely. When the trigger is pulled, it lifts the spring up, which in turn lifts the cord off the tin notch.

The stick for the bow, *Figure 4*, is dressed down from a point ¾ in. on each side of the centerline to ½ in. wide at each end. Notches are cut in the ends for the cord. The bow is not fastened in the stock, it is wrapped with a piece of canvas 1½ in. wide on the centerline to make a tight fit in the mortise. A stout cord is now tied in the notches cut in the ends of the bow making the cord taut when the wood is straight.

The design of the arrows is shown in *Figure 5* and they are made with the blades much thinner than the round part.

To shoot the crossbow, pull the cord back and down in the notch as shown in *Figure 6*, place the arrow in the groove, sight and pull the trigger as in shooting an ordinary gun.

The arrow sling is made form a branch of ash about ½ in. in diameter, the bark removed and a notch cut in one end, as shown in *Figure 7*. A stout cord about 2½ ft. long is tied in the notch and a large knot made in the other or loose end. The arrows are practically the same as those used on the crossbow, with the exception of a small notch that is cut in them as shown in *Figure 8*.

To throw the arrow, insert the cord near the knot in the notch of the arrow, then grasping the stick with the right hand and holding the wing of the arrow with the left, as shown in *Figure 9,* throw the arrow with a quick, slinging motion. The arrow may be thrown several hundred feet after a little practice.

{ CHAPTER 6 }

CAMPFIRE GRUB

HOME *on the* RANGE

— A SIMPLE CAMP STOVE —

Finding that a mixture of earth and gasoline would burn with a fine hot flame, even if the earth were wet, an ingenious camper devised the simple portable camp stove shown in the drawing. It consists of a wide, shallow tin can having a row of holes punched through the side along the upper edge. The can is about half filled with earth, then about ¼ pint of gasoline is poured over the

A VERY SIMPLE BUT EFFICIENT FORM OF GASOLINE CAMP OR TOURING STOVE.

earth and thoroughly mixed with it. Upon lighting this mixture, it burns with an intense heat for about fifteen minutes, which is ample time for preparing coffee. Three tin cans, one a little smaller than the other so that they can be telescoped into each other to save space when carrying, have been found very convenient on camping trips.

— CAMP STOVE IMPROVISED FROM PAIL —

You need only a 5-pound lard pail and an empty can to make a good outdoor stove. Punch a number of holes in the pail, then put a few pebbles in the small can to weight it down. Fill it with either gasoline or wood alcohol and set it inside the pail. Ignite the fuel and place your cooking utensils on top of the pail, which acts both as a holder for the utensils, and a windbreak for the fire.

— IMPROVISED "CAMP STOVE" SMOTHERS FIRE —

To avoid starting forest fires by careless handling of a campfire, one sportsman recommends this stove for campers who stay only a short time in one place. It consists of two or more iron rods supported on rolls of sod, which are turned back to provide a bare spot for the fire. When finished with the fire, the rods are removed and the sod is rolled back into place, covering the coals and effectually smothering all flames or sparks that may remain.

Outdoor Fireplace Covered with Top of Old Stove —

Before building an outdoor fireplace for a permanent camp, get the top from an old iron cook stove to use as a cover. Then put up the fireplace to fit it. With the stove top, the heat is even on all parts of the cooking surface, smoke goes up the chimney of the fireplace, and pots and pans are protected from the soot and blaze of the fire. Cook stoves or tops of old stoves can usually be picked up in the country or at a local junk shop for almost nothing.

— A Convenient Campfire Hob —

Crude methods of holding pots and kettles over the campfire usually cause more inconvenience in preparing food, but such trouble can be avoided by providing a campfire hob.

The hob is made of pipe and fittings and can easily be carried along in the automobile, because it is small and weighs only about seven pounds. It consists of a post that is driven into the ground almost its entire length, and a revolving crane fitted with cooking arms to hold such units as grid, grate, and pot hooks. The post is a 24-in. length of ¾-in. pipe with a hole drilled through it about 3 in. from the upper end. This allows a heavy spike to be pushed through to serve as a rest for the crane, which is set into the end, and also as a handle to pull the post out of the ground when breaking camp.

The crane is made of lengths of ⅜-in. pipe and fittings. It consists of one 13-in. length of pipe with tees screwed on both ends, and shorter extending lengths to support a

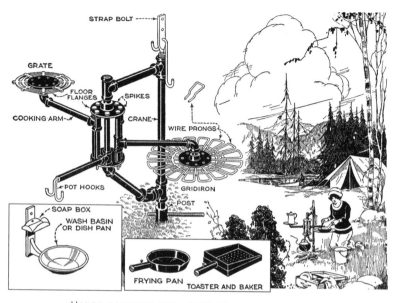

HANDY CAMPFIRE HOB, MADE OF PIPE AND FITTINGS,
WEIGHS ABOUT SEVEN POUNDS AND CAN EASILY
BE CARRIED IN THE AUTO. THE LOWER DETAILS
SUGGEST A FEW HANDY COOKING UTENSILS.

revolving hob to which the cooking arms are attached. A 4-in. nipple is screwed into the bottom tee on the crane to fit into the top of the post.

The hob is mounted between the two arms as shown. It consists of two large floor flanges with holes drilled near the edges to accommodate large spikes, which are slipped through the ¼-in. pipe nipples of various lengths. These fit loosely between the flanges and are fitted with tees

that hold cooking arms extending at right angles.

A grate is attached to one of the cooking arms. The grate is simply an ordinary gas-stove grate or similar contrivance bolted to a floor flange. A gridiron is attached to another cooking arm; it consists of another gas-stove grate, also attached to a flange and fitted with a number of wire prongs, bent to the shape shown. The pot hooks are made of

No. 10 galvanized-iron wire, pushed into the end of an arm. A strap bolt fitted with a wire hanger is provided on top of the crane for the purpose of hanging up cooking utensils, a washbasin and the like. Both grate and gridiron elbows are fastened to the arms with pins so that they can be used either side up.

Although every camper has his own idea as to which cooking utensils are handiest, the lower details in the drawing suggest some useful ones. A dustpan from which the paint and varnish have been burned and with the bottom perforated, makes an excellent toaster and baker. It is fitted with an extra perforated bottom of sheet metal, bent over and riveted to the sides. A common frying pan is also used, with an extension made from a piece of sheet metal riveted to the handle. The arm tees for these units must be pinned so that they cannot turn over accidentally. The detail at the left shows a washbasin mounted on a bracket that can be hung on the strap bolt.

— QUICK AND EASY CAMP STOVES —

The camp stoves illustrated are different forms of the same idea. Both can be taken apart and laid flat for packing. Iron rods, ½ in. in diameter, are used for the legs. They are sharpened at the lower end so

CAMP-STOVE TOP, EITHER SOLID OR PIECED, SUPPORTED ON RODS AT THE CORNERS

that they may be easily driven into the ground. The rods of the one shown in the first illustration are bent in the form of a hook at the upper end, and two pieces of light tire iron, with holes in either end, are hung on these hooks.

Across these supports are laid other pieces of the tire iron. In the other stove, the rods have large heads and are slipped through holes in the four corners of the piece of heavy sheet iron used for the top. A cotter pin is slipped through a hole in each rod just below the top, to hold the latter in place.

CAMP KITCHEN GADGETS

— TWIG HOLDS SANDWICH PLATE, LEAVING HANDS FREE —

The next time you are having a picnic lunch at the campsite, you can keep both hands free by supporting your plate on a sharpened twig, pushed into the ground. The plate is punctured so that it can be slipped over the twig and is supported on two or three cut-off sprigs.

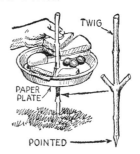

— A BIRCH-BARK BERRYING BASKET —

A simple berrying basket can be easily improvised in the woods, when a regular basket or bag is not available. Tear a strip of bark from a birch tree, and fold it over, as shown in the photo. Fold in the edges at the side and bottom, and "sew" them together with a slender flexible green twig. Attach another piece of twig to the top of the basket, to serve as a handle. This basket is quite strong, considering its rough construction, and serves very well for the purpose of carrying berries, fruits, and nuts. It can, of course, be made any size desired.

— A NUT-CRACKING BLOCK —

A secret treasure greets the camper who makes his camp in the woods near fruit and nut trees. A cache of walnuts can make wonderful snacks for a hike, but getting to the meat of the nut can be a hard task indeed. In the sketch herewith is shown an appliance for cracking nuts that will prevent many a bruised thumb. To anyone who has ever tried to crack butternuts it needs no further recommendation. The device is nothing more than good block of hardwood with a few holes bored in it to fit the different sized nuts. There is no need of holding the nut with the fingers, and as hard a blow may be struck as desired.

HOLES IN BLOCK FOR NUTS.

Make the depth of the hole two-thirds the height of the nut and the broken pieces will not scatter.

— SIX WIENERS ROASTED ON A WIRE HOLDER —

Instead of impaling a wiener on a pointed stick and roasting one at a time, use a wire holder like the one shown and save time. There will be enough "spring" in the bent wire to grip six wieners firmly, and there is no possibility of the holder burning off and dropping the wiener into the fire. With two or three of these holders, wieners for a large group can be roasted.

3' LENGTH OF No. 9 WIRE

— TIN CAN ON ROD FOR PICKING FRUIT —

The best apple is usually a little beyond reach, as every boy knows. So a hungry camper fitted a tin can, cut as shown in the sketch, to a pole to easily pick the apple that he wanted. The device is useful for picking many varieties of fruit, and prevents damaging the fruit by a fall. This tin-can fruit picker is especially handy for picking apples or other fruit from the upper branches of trees, where it is almost impossible to reach with a ladder. The small sketch shows how the edge of the can should be cut to afford the best grip on the stem, making it possible to cut the twig from above or below.

THE OPEN-AIR FEAST

— PICNIC CLOTH SECURED BY CLOTHESPIN —

When having a picnic away from the campsite, sharpen five or six regular clothespins and take them along. They are ideal for anchoring the corners of the luncheon cloth to the ground to keep wind from blowing it about. Just twist each corner of the cloth, insert it between the legs of a clothespin and push the clothespin into the ground at an angle as indicated in the circular detail.

— KEEPING ANTS OUT OF THE LUNCH BOX —

If you have had ants get in your lunch box, here is a hanger that will keep them out. It is nothing more than a length of heavy wire with hooks bent on both ends and compression can lid soldered in the center. After you hang up the box as shown in the photo, fill the can lid with water. If ants crawl down the upper part of the hanger, they will not cross the water to reach the box.

— SCREW EYE REMOVES CAPS —

If you are camping out and have forgotten a bottle-cap remover, one can be improvised from a screw eye. Usually a screw eye can be found in a car tool kits.

Open the eye and drive the screw into a board. If a file is available, bevel the end of the eye so it will slip under the edge of the cap.

— COOKING IN CAMP WITHOUT DISHES —

You can broil a fish in camp without cooking utensils. After cleaning and seasoning it, place it on a flat rock that has been made blistering hot. There will be enough heat in the average stone to cook both sides without reheating. Another good way to prepare fish is to clean, season, and then wrap them in large catalpa leaves. The fish can be covered with cornmeal first if desired. A well-seasoned fish covered with a mud batter from deep clay and water, if cooked in hot ashes for 20 minutes, will be about as tasty as though it were broiled in an oven. Potatoes, eggs and other foods can be baked in clay coverings.

A large bird may be roasted over an open fire if it is first impaled on a long, slender stick suspended by crotched stakes on each side of the fire, then turned slowly while it is cooking.

— How to Make Popcorn Cakes —

Popcorn balls can be light-weight treats to take on a camping excursion, but it is very difficult to take a bite from a ball of popcorn, and it becomes more difficult as the ball increases in size. As a large number of balls were required for a campout, so the camper decided to make the popcorn into cakes. This was more easily accomplished than first imagined with the use of a cake-forming device as shown in the illustration. The body of the former was made of a baking-powder can with the bottom removed. The cover of the can was nailed to the top of an old table with its flange upward. A plunger of wood was made to fit snugly inside of the can and a lever, about 3 ft. long, attached to it and fulcrumed to the wall.

After the popcorn had been prepared with the syrup, it was placed in the can and compressed. The plunger was then lifted out of the cover and the popcorn cake removed. This method offered a much better way to serve popcorn than in balls. In making the cakes, the can, cover, and plunger must be kept well covered with butter.

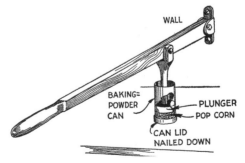

POPCORN BALLS, WHEN FORMED INTO CAKES ABOUT ONE INCH THICK, ARE MORE EASILY HANDLED.

— Keeping Food Cool in Camps —

Camps and suburban homes located where ice is hard to get can be provided with a cooling arrangement herein described that will make a good substitute for the icebox. A barrel is sunk in the ground in a shady place, allowing plenty of space about the outside to fill in with gravel. A quantity of small stones and sand is first put in wet. A box is placed in the hole over the top of the barrel and filled in with clay or earth well-tamped. The porous condition of the gravel drains the surplus water after a rain.

The end of the barrel is fitted with a light cover and a heavy door hinged to the box. A small portion of damp sand is sprinkled on the bottom of the barrel. The covers should be left open occasionally to prevent mold and to remove any bad air that may have collected from the contents.

Outdoor Kitchen Appliances

— Campers' Water Canteen —

While on a summer's camping trip and using a small tent having a sewed-in floor cloth, a camper experienced some trouble with the water canteen during sultry nights. Sometimes the stopper of the water bottle became dislodged through the unconscious movements of the sleeper, and it was often a problem how to stow this

RUBBER TUBE SUPPLIED CAMPER WITH WATER INSIDE OF TENT FROM OUTSIDE CANTEEN.

equipment so that there would be no danger of spilling water on the blanket, yet have the water handy. The drawing shows how the problem was solved. The barrel was simply placed outside of the tent and a length of rubber tubing used as siphon. A leather washer sewed both inside and outside, around the hole in the tent, prevented wear on the canvas.

— AN EFFICIENT ICE BOX FOR THE CAMP OR COTTAGE —

You need have no worries about food spoilage at your camp if this icebox is used. The secret of its efficiency lies in its adequate insulation and close-fitting lid, which has an air-cooled top as further protection if the box must be exposed to the sun on an open area. Construction is simple. The only extra precaution necessary is to see that the lid fits perfectly. Note that the sills "A" are nailed flush with the bottom, and corner pieces "B" and "C" rest on them.

After filling the hollow walls with insulating board and crumpled paper, the piece "D" is applied to seal the compartment. Do not shred the paper, but tear it in half sheets so that air pockets will be formed.

— FOLDING PICNIC TABLE IN CAR STORES YOUR FOOD AND DISHES —

Crawling insects, damp ground and other inconveniences will not detract from the enjoyment of a campground picnic lunch if you have this cabinet in your car. It fits snugly on the back of the front seat and does not reduce foot room. Inside the cabinet you can pack all the necessary things for a picnic lunch where they are out of the way and protected from sun and dust. When a place to park is found, lift the lid that covers part of the cabinet front and it serves as a table. Beneath the lid are two drawers that can be removed and taken into the "kitchen" when the lunch is being made up, thus doing away with a cumbersome hamper. Another advantage is that things placed in the drawers remain right side up.

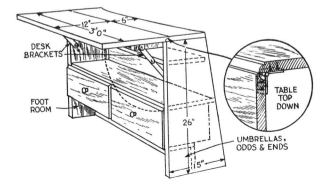

— FOLDING CAMP KITCHEN —

In this compact camp kitchen everything is in reach of the chef. When folded, it is 19 in. deep, 30 in. high, and 36 in. long, permitting it to be carried on the running board or in the rear compartment of an automobile. As shown in the drawing, the legs fold up under the table, which drops flat against the back of the cupboard. The covers of the

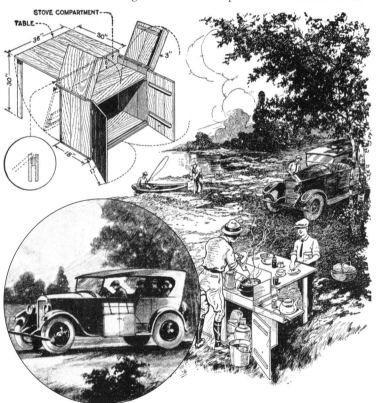

FOLDING CAMPERS' KITCHEN, WHICH
CAN BE CARRIED ON THE RUNNING BOARD.

stove compartment swing out to the side and form handy shelves. The cupboard may be partitioned and provided with shelves to suit the individual taste. A few hooks for dishcloths, pans, etc., will increase its convenience.

The outfit is so simple that anyone can construct it easily with ordinary tools. All dimensions are based on the use of a ½-in. lumber throughout. Hinges that fold flat should be used in all cases and folding parts provided with hooks to hold them in place when closed. A grab handle should be placed on each end of the cupboard to facilitate carrying. The stove shelf, and all others, are set back ½ in. from the front to allow the cupboard doors to close. The table legs are spaced so that they will lie edge-to-edge when folded inward, and the table is hinged to the back of the cupboard as shown in the enlarged detail.

— Refrigerator for the Camp —

An excellent refrigerator for the camp or summer cottage can readily be made by lining a wooden dry-goods box with galvanized iron, and soldering all seams, so as to make it watertight. This refrigerator can also serve as a drinking tank.

The refrigerator has three compartments: the large one is used for the drinking water, the one at the left in the photograph for cream and milk bottles, and the smallest one for meats and vegetables. The two large compartments are made by making a

A WOODEN DRY-GOODS BOX, LINED WITH GALVANIZED IRON AND DIVIDED INTO SEVERAL COMPARTMENTS, MAKES AN EXCELLENT REFRIGERATOR FOR THE CAMP.

partition across the box, but the smaller one is simply a removable galvanized iron box. The compartments can be made any size.

Water from a spring is led into the box by means of a length of pipe, and flows from the main compartment into the smaller one through a hole drilled in the partition. A drain hole is drilled in the outer side of the second compartment so that the surplus water will flow out. This hole is drilled at about two-thirds the height of quart-size milk bottles. The hole in the partition may be higher than this, so that the level of the water in the largest compartment will reach nearly to the top of the small meat box.

It has been found a refrigerator of this type, about 3 ft. by 18 in., by 12 in. in dimensions, will keep milk and cream sweet for three days during the hottest weather.

INDEX